ABBA FATHER

ABBA FATHER

THE LORD'S PATTERN FOR PRAYER

R. Kent Hughes

Foreword by James M. Boice

Crossway Books • Wheaton, Illinois
A DIVISION OF GOOD NEWS PUBLISHERS

For
my daughters
Holly and Heather,
the joy of their fathers
on Earth
and in Heaven

CONTENTS

*God has sent forth the Spirit of His Son
into our hearts, crying, "Abba! Father!"*
(Galatians 4:6)

FOREWORD

by James Montgomery Boice

O urs is a day of big things but small minds, of great technology but little deep or sustained thought. This should not be true in Christian circles, of course, but it is. So it is particularly pleasing when a work comes along that helps us stretch our thought along Biblical and theological lines.

Kent Hughes' informative yet readable study of the Lord's Prayer is such a work.

It is strange that so few in our day have put serious time into understanding and applying this prayer, for in earlier ages of the church it was recognized, almost instinctively, that it is an important portion of the Word of God and deserves deep study. More than that, it provides a model for that most essential part of every Christian's personal walk with God—namely, prayer. In earlier days the Lord's Prayer was regularly expounded as part of every church's catechism. In the Westminster Shorter Catechism, for instance, the last nine questions deal with the Lord's Prayer: "What rule hath God given for our direction in prayer?," "What doth the preface of the Lord's Prayer teach us?," "What do we pray for in the first petition?" and so on.

This study of the Lord's model for His follower's prayers is not a catechism, but it does make up a lack in this area and will prove useful to many persons. It is exegetically accurate, theologically sound and, above all, practical—as only a pastor who works with his people and loves them can be. I think you will enjoy reading it, as I have.

INTRODUCTION

T he Lord's Prayer has been, and remains, the greatest prayer of the church. The church's best minds have consistently treated it so and have used it to preach countless sermons on prayer and basic Christian doctrine.

In the early church, such notables as Origen, Gregory of Nyssa, Tertullian, Cyril of Jerusalem, and Cyprian published expositions of the Lord's Prayer. Later, the greatest of the ancient theologians, Augustine, followed suit. Dante devoted the eleventh canto of the *Purgatorio* to the Lord's Prayer. Meister Eckhart, the medieval Dominican mystic and theologian, used the categories of the Lord's Prayer to sum up scholastic theology.

Martin Luther preached a volume of exposition on the Lord's Prayer. And the famous Westminster Catechism of the Presbyterian churches bases its last nine questions on the Lord's Prayer.[1] The Lord's Prayer is without a doubt the greatest prayer of the Christian church.

This great prayer has been called the Lord's

Prayer for almost two thousand years. So it would be futile to attempt to change its name—though the best title really would be "The Disciples' Prayer," because that is what it is. At the disciples' request (Luke 11:1), Jesus provided it for them as a pattern for prayer.

Strictly speaking, it is a prayer that the sinless Christ could never pray in its entirety, because the last part includes a petition for the forgiveness of sins: *"forgive us our debts, as we also have forgiven our debtors."* But the outline with its six petitions is absolutely perfect for every man or woman who has ever lived.

The initial focus of this model prayer is upward, as its first three requests have to do with God's glory. Then, having prayed for His glory, the remaining three requests are for our well-being. God first, humans second. That is the ideal order of prayer: His glory before our wants.

In this respect this prayer is like another of the great documents of the Scriptures, the Ten Commandments, the first four of which have to do with God's glory and the last six with humanity's well-being (Exodus 20:1-17).

The Lord's Prayer is the perfect prayer. Of its perfection Dietrich Bonhoeffer said:

> The Lord's Prayer is not merely the pattern prayer, it is the way Christians must pray. . . .
> The Lord's Prayer is the quintessence of prayer.[2]

It is the perfect pattern for the followers of Christ, and its depth cannot be exhausted by exposition. No matter how one advances in the matter of prayer, it remains the model and the challenge.

But the sad irony is that the Lord's Prayer is more often mindlessly repeated than prayed. Each Sunday morning in countless churches, more people "say" the Lord's Prayer than pray it. This is especially ironic because the context that introduces the Lord's Prayer in Matthew 6:7, 8 warns against meaningless repetition: "And when you are praying," Jesus says, "do not use meaningless repetition, as the Gentiles do. . . ." The obvious problem for all of us is that "familiarity breeds contempt," or more appropriately here, "surface familiarity breeds contempt." Some of us learned the Lord's Prayer at a tender age. We cannot count the times we have repeated it. We repeated it as children. We repeat it today as adults. The Lord's Prayer is one of the beautiful things of our life. But there is a danger in our familiarity with its beauty. It can become just beautiful words—so that we, too, "say" the Lord's Prayer without actually praying.

There are probably people who live in the mountains of Colorado who rarely "see" the incredible scenery that occupies their every glance. Meanwhile, flatlanders travel a thousand miles just to view the mountains' beauty for a few days—and they really see it! Those who have been dulled to beauty need to see things in a new way. So also in respect to the Lord's Prayer. The best thing to do is to see it anew—not so much in discovering new truth, but in seeing the old truth for what it is.

My hope for this book is to heighten the underlying, foundational awareness with which we must pray. I believe that an in-depth study of the Lord's Prayer can do just that—as it has for thousands over the centuries.

1

GOD
THE FATHER

We begin with the first six English words, *"Our Father who art in heaven"*—for they state the primary awareness with which we must pray—that God is our Father.

Our *Father*

That God should be personally addressed as "Father" may not seem out of the ordinary to those of us who frequent the church and pray the Lord's Prayer, but it was absolutely revolutionary in Jesus' day. The writers of the Old Testament certainly believed in the Fatherhood of God, but they saw it mainly in terms of a sovereign Creator-Father to whom they owed their paternity.

In fact, God is only referred to as Father fourteen times in the huge corpus of the Old Testament's thirty-nine books—and then rather impersonally. In those fourteen occurrences of "Father," the term was always used with reference to the nation, and not individuals. God was spoken of as Israel's Father, but Abraham did not speak of God as "my

Father." You can search from Genesis to Malachi, and you will not find such an occurrence.

Moreover, in Jesus' day, His contemporaries had so focused on the sovereignty and transcendence of God that they were careful never to repeat His covenant name, "Jahweh," and so invented the word "Jehovah," which was made of a combination of two separate names of God. Thus, the distance from God was well guarded.

But when Jesus came on the scene, He addressed God only as Father. He never used anything else. All His prayers address God as Father. The Gospels (just four books) record His using Father more than sixty times in reference to God. So striking is this that some scholars maintain that this word "Father" dramatically capsulizes the difference between the Old Testament and New Testament. No one had ever in the entire history of Israel spoken and prayed like Jesus. No one!

But this amazing fact is only part of the story, because the word Jesus used for Father was not a formal word. It was the common Aramaic word with which a child would address its father—the word "Abba." The great German New Testament scholar Joachim Jeremias, perhaps the most respected New Testament scholar of his generation, has argued convincingly that "Abba" was the original word on Jesus' lips here in the Lord's Prayer and, indeed, in all of His prayers in the New Testament—with the exception of Matthew 27:46

when He cried out from the cross, "My God, my God, why hast Thou Forsaken Me?" But there, Jeremias explains, Jesus was quoting Psalm 22:1.[1] Jesus reverted to "Father" with the final words before His death: "Father, into Thy hands I commit My spirit" (Luke 23:46, quoting Psalm 31:5).

The word "Abba" was also the word Jesus regularly used to address His earthly father, Joseph, from the time Jesus was a baby until Joseph's death. Everyone used the word; but as the careful examination of other literature of the time shows, it was never used of God—under any circumstances. "Abba" meant something like "Daddy"—but with a more reverent touch than we use it. The best rendering is "Dearest Father."

To the traditional Jew, Jesus' prayer was revolutionary. Think of it. God was referred to only fourteen times in the Old Testament as "Father," and then it was as the corporate Father of Israel—never the individual or personal Father. Now, as His disciples ask Him for instruction on how to pray, Jesus enjoins them to begin by calling God their Father, their "Abba"! As Jeremias says,

. . . in the Lord's Prayer Jesus authorizes His disciples to repeat the word *abba* after Him. He gives them a share in His sonship and empowers them, as His disciples, to speak with their heavenly Father in just such a familiar, trusting way as a child would with his father.[2]

When we say "Abba" today in our prayers, as we sometimes do, we are making the same sound that actually fell from Jesus' lips—and the lips of His incredulous disciples. Jesus transformed the relationship with God from a distant, corporate experience into an intimate, one-to-one bond, and He taught His disciples to pray with the same intimacy. And that is what He does for us.

The way we are to pray is *"Our Father"*—"Our Abba"—"Our Dearest Father." This is to be the foundational awareness of all of our prayer. We must honestly ask ourselves if this awareness pervades our prayer life. And then we must go further and ask ourselves if the sense of God's intimate Fatherhood is profound and growing.

The impulse to address God as "Abba" (Dearest Father) is not only an indication of our spiritual health, but is a mark of the authenticity of our faith. Paul tells us in Galatians 4:6: "And because you are sons, God has sent forth the Spirit of His Son into our hearts, crying, 'Abba! Father!'" The impulse is the sign of being God's child. Romans 8:15, 16 says the same: ". . . but you have received a spirit of adoption as sons by which we cry out, 'Abba! Father!' The Spirit Himself bears witness with our spirit that we are children of God."

True believers are impelled to say this.

This is precisely what happened to me when I came to faith during the summer before my freshman year in high school. Before that I had a cool theological idea of the universal paternity of God as the Creator of all humanity. His Fatherhood was there, but it was not personal. Then, with my conversion, God became warm and personal, and "Dear Father" the constant refrain of my subconscious. I knew God, and I knew He was my Father!

This realization is one of the great and primary works of the Holy Spirit. His work is to make Christians realize with increasing clarity the meaning of their filial relationship with God in Christ. He keeps enhancing this "spirit of adoption" in us and is ever integrating it into our lives.

Let me ask a personal question of each one of us. Do we have a "spirit of adoption"? Do we sense that God is our Father? Do we think of Him, and address Him, as our "Dear Father"? If we cannot answer in the affirmative, it may be because He is not our spiritual Father; and, therefore, we need to heed the words of Scripture and receive Him. "But as many as received Him, to them He gave the right to become children of God, even to those who believe in His name" (John 1:12).

Dr. J. I. Packer considers one's grasp of God's Fatherhood and one's adoption as a son or daughter as of essential importance to spiritual life. He says:

If you want to judge how well a person understands Christianity, find out how much he makes of the thought of being God's child, and having God as his father. If this is not the thought that prompts and controls his worship and prayers and his whole outlook on life, it means that he does not understand Christianity very well at all. For everything that Christ taught, everything that makes the New Testament new, and better than the Old, everything that is distinctively Christian as opposed to merely Jewish, is summed up in the knowledge of the Fatherhood of God. "Father" is the Christian name for God.[3]

That God is our Abba-Father is a truth that we must cultivate for the sake of our soul's health.

The Father-child understanding brings wholeness to spiritual life. First, it brings a sense of being loved. Reverend Everett Fullam tells how this came home to him when he was ministering to a remote tribe of people in Nigeria. The tribe was so isolated that it had never heard the word Africa, much less America. They had a prescientific view of creation, so simplistic that when Fullam mentioned to the chief the then-recent phenomenon of two Americans walking on the moon, the old chief looked hard into Fullam's face, and then up at the moon, and exclaimed in an angry tone, "There's nobody up there! Besides, it is not big enough for two people to stand on."

The old chief meant it. He had absolutely no idea of the size of the moon or its distance from the earth. But it was there in the wilds of west Africa that Fullam had the memorable experience which drove home to him what it means to know God as

Father. The moment came when he was invited to baptize three converts, people who had come to know the love of God through faith in Jesus Christ, although they, like the old chief, knew little about science and the universe. Fullam describes his experience this way:

> There were two men and one woman. We stood on the banks of a muddy river, wet and happy. I had never seen three more joyful people. "What is the best thing about this experience?" I asked. All three continued to smile, the glistening water emphasizing the brightness of their dark-skinned faces; but only one spoke, in clear, deliberate English: "Behind this universe stands one God, not a great number of warring spirits, as we had always believed, but one God. And that God loves me."[4]

How beautiful! Separated by millennia of culture, men and women through faith in Christ found the same spirit of adoption and the same sense of God's intimate love that we also find through Christ. Those three tribespeople now prayed, "Our Father," and experienced the same sense of love that we know.

Next, the sense of God's Fatherhood helps drive home the reality of our forgiveness. The word "Father" implies forgiveness. I think it is most significant that the first word to fall from the Prodigal Son's lips when he returned was "Father." "Father,

I have sinned against heaven and in your sight . . ."
(Luke 15:21). And, of course, those words were followed by forgiveness. The more deep-seated our
sense of God's tender, loving care, the deeper will
be our sense of forgiveness and the wholeness that
comes from being loved and forgiven.

Then there is also the confidence and security it
gives us. When I was a young father and my children were very small, my younger son once hid on
top of the refrigerator. As I walked by, with no
warning he suddenly dove off the refrigerator onto
my back. I didn't see him, I didn't feel him coming—he just tackled me and held on. And I held
him up.

As I thought about it later, I realized that Carey
felt that if he jumped in the direction of his father,
he was going to be safe. He might have knocked
me silly, but it never occurred to him that I would
not catch him. That is the way it is with our Abba,
our Heavenly Father. He gives us a great sense of
security and confidence—and it is a valid sense of
security and confidence.

My point is this: the concept that God is our
Father, our Abba, is not only a sign of our spiritual
health and the authenticity of our faith, but it is one
of the most healing doctrines of all of Scripture.
Some have never had a positive relationship with
an earthly father. There are entire neighborhoods in
our large cities where there are almost no fathers—
just mothers and children. In such situations, the

experience of knowing a caring father is rare. There are also thousands who have grown up in conventional homes with fathers where the relationship with father or mother was negative at best. The fact is, whatever our background, we need the touch of a loving parent. Our Lord wants to provide that. That is another reason why He commands all of us to pray "Our Father"—"Our Dearest Abba Father." If we need to, we can simply say, "Dearest Father," "Abba," and find the wholeness and healing that God wants to give us.

Our Father, *Who Art in Heaven*

As we have seen, Jesus' use of "Father" and "Abba" to address God was amazingly revolutionary because the Jewish theology of the time stressed the transcendence and sovereignty of God—that He was so far above and so "other" that He could not be addressed with familiarity.

On the other hand, the problem today among some evangelical Christians is reversed, because they have sentimentalized God so that He has been robbed of His holiness. Many Christians are flippantly sentimental about God and sing tunes about the "great big God in the sky" as if He were some big celestial teddy bear.

Such songs may not actually be blasphemous—but they come very close. Moreover, such flip familiarity—which outwardly suggests exceptional intimacy with God—really points to shallowness and a defective knowledge of God.

Jesus provides the remedy to both errors with His opening words, *"Our Father, who art in heaven."* *"Father"* stresses God's immanence: He is involved in life and is to be intimately approached as Abba. *"Who art in heaven"* stresses God's transcendence: He surpasses all that is human; He is sovereign and reigning. In a word, He is our Father and our King. We are to affectionately call Him "Abba," "Dear Father," perhaps even "Daddy," but we do it with a deep sense of wonder and reverence.

He is our Father, but He is not restricted to the analogy of our earthly parents. He exceeds them in all their nurturing and protecting qualities because He is *"Our Father . . . in heaven."* He always understands. He always is caring and loving. He never forgets. And He always delivers.

This is the way little children regard their fathers. I well remember the day that one of my boys came in with his little buddy, Greggie Salazar, saying, "You can beat up Mr. Salazar, can't you, Dad? Greggie says you can't." And he kept repeating this while I kept saying, "Don't talk so loud—shh!" Each boy *knew* his father was the stronger and could deliver.

There is no doubt about our Heavenly Father, because He is "our Father in heaven." He is superior. He exceeds all of our earthly fathers' virtues one billion-fold. Oh, the tenderness and power that the opening lines of the Lord's Prayer evoke!

Our Father

The Prayer begins with the word *"Our"*—*"Our Father."* "Our" is the pronoun of partnership. While it is beneficial sometimes to say, "My Father," Jesus purposely says, "Our," because he wants to stress the identity that God's Fatherhood brings.

When we pray the Lord's Prayer, we are affirming that we are brothers and sisters, and that if we love God, we must love one another. There is no place in God's family for the much-glorified American individualism which says, "I don't need anyone else—and they don't need me." *"Our Father"* calls us not only upward, but outward to minister to our brothers and sisters as members of our own family. The Fatherhood of God enriches life vertically and horizontally. How beautiful His ways and His words are!

What is the foundational awareness with which we are to pray? It is that God is our tender, loving Father, our Abba; He loves us like a parent; He forgives us like a parent; He takes care of us like a parent. The other part of the awareness is that He can deliver, for He is "Our Father . . . in heaven." He exceeds every virtue of our earthly parents.

And, finally, all this suggests how we ought to pray. There are three ways: first, with confidence. When my children come to me saying, as my girls sometimes do, "Daddy, dear," they make my day. And it is my delight to do anything for them which is in reason. In the same way, God delights in answering our prayers. We may, we must, be confident.

Secondly, we must pray with simplicity. Fathers do not look for eloquent rhetoric from their children—just simple, direct, heartfelt conversation. Let us honor God with our simplicity.

Lastly, we ought to pray with love. The words "Abba, Father" are the words of love, and our prayer ought to be overflowing with love. "Our Father, who art in heaven, we love You. Amen."

2

GOD's NAME

Those who have the occasion to visit Hawaii will soon learn a new word, if they do not already know it. The word is *haoli*—which is the word Hawaiians use for those from the mainland. Though often spoken today without any malice, it was once used with withering disdain. Alice Kahokuoluna gives the derivation of the term:

> Before the missionaries came, my people used to sit outside their temples for a long time meditating and preparing themselves before entering. Then they would virtually creep to the altar to offer their petition and afterwards would again sit a long time outside, this time to "breathe life" into their prayers. The Christians, when they came, just got up, uttered a few sentences, said Amen and were done. For that reason my people call them *haolis*, "without breath," or those who fail to breathe life into their prayers.[1]

Just how deserved this biting religious reproach was is subject to question, because missionaries are often misrepresented by unsympathetic historians. But, however that may be, *haoli* well describes the condition of multitudes of today's Christians who live life in the "fast lane"—dashing into God's presence, uttering some empty conventionalities, pausing to make a few requests (unless they are really in trouble!), and then stepping back into the rush—while never pausing to breathe life into their prayers. *Haolis* in the fullest sense of the word.

The problem is extensive, as we all know. I think one of the great sins of modern Christianity is that we are spiritual *haolis*.

The remedy for this is found in Christ's pattern for prayer, as He gave it to the disciples in the Lord's Prayer. The foundational awareness that the opening words, *"Our Father, who art in Heaven,"* impose on us demands that we take time to breathe life into our prayers.

Many of us would do well to follow the custom of some of the Old Testament saints, who would prepare themselves before their prayer time by reflecting on whom they were going to speak to. This is something which I often do before my own prayer times; and I have found it to make a great difference in the way I pray. I think about Him, His Fatherhood, His omnipresence, His omniscience, His love—to focus on Him, to breathe life into my prayers before I go to prayer.

Now, having the foundational awareness contained in the words, *"Our Father, who art in heaven,"* we move to the *foundational petition: "Hallowed be Thy name."* As we have noted, the prayer is divided into six petitions. Three are for God: *"Thy name," "Thy kingdom," "Thy will."* And three are for us: *"Give us," "forgive us," "lead us not . . . but deliver us."* This foundational petition is placed first by divine intention, because it interprets and controls what follows.

The Upward, Godward Aspect of the Foundational Petition

It is highly significant that this foundational petition is upward—*"Hallowed be Thy name."* The God-given order for prayer is first in regard to God. To be sure, there are times when prayer in regard to our own needs is all we can do—as when Peter cried, "Lord, save me!" (Matthew 14:30) as he was sinking below the waves. That wasn't the time for worship! Worship came very soon, however. To insist that all prayer begin with the pattern of the Lord's prayer is, in fact, a denial of what *"Our Father"* means to us. Nevertheless, the normal prayer is to begin with a loving upward rush of the heart to God. Let us consider the petition, the meaning of which rests on two words, *"Hallowed"* and *"name."*

First, the meaning of *"name."* Today names do not mean much more to us than convenient labels to identify people by. We commonly say, "A rose by any other name would smell as sweet." Perhaps some of us will think about what a name means when we name our children. But often a bigger concern is that the name be euphonious, or that it honor some relative.

But for the Jew, a name was anything but a convenient label, because names were considered to indicate character. This especially applied to the name of God. The Psalmist said (20:7): "Some boast in chariots, and some of horses; but we will boast in the name [the character] of the Lord, our God." For the Jew, God's name referred to the reality of God. This was the Semitic way of thinking.

God's names were, therefore, revelatory of His being. For instance, we have the list of Jehovah combinations: Jehovah Shalom, "the Lord of our Peace," was a name which Gideon hallowed by raising an altar to God by that name. Jehovah Jireh, "the Lord will provide," was the name by which Abraham came to know God on Mt. Moriah when God provided the ram in place of Isaac. Jehovah Tsidkenu, "the Lord our Righteousness," was the name by which God revealed Himself to Jeremiah in the captivity. The list of names is quite long: Jehovah-nissi, El Shaddai, El Elyon, Adonai—and all reflect His character.

What is the name that is prominent here in the Lord's Prayer? Very simply, but very profoundly, it is His name "Father"—"Abba, Father." The context demands this understanding. "Our Father who

art in heaven, hallowed be Thy name as Father."
The name that we ask to be *hallowed* is Dearest
Father.

What does it mean to "hallow" His name? The
word *"hallow"* means "to set apart as holy"—"to
consider holy"—"to treat as holy." The best alter-
native term is "to reverence." *"Hallowed"* means:
"May You be given that unique reverence that
Your character and nature as Father demand." St.
Chrysostom had the same idea when he said it included the idea of honor, and Calvin agreed, saying
it called for the greatest veneration.[2]

This petition, that His name as "Dear Father"
be made holy or be reverenced, has two distinct
times in mind. First, eternity, when in a final event
His Fatherhood will be fully revealed before all creation. (Note: This is what the *aorist tense* makes primary, as Ernst Lohmeyer shows in his *Our Father,*
Harper & Row, 1965, p. 81.) Second, that God's
name be hallowed in the present fallen age. This is
exactly what Jesus did, in His own ministry, as He
told His Father in John 17:25, 26a: "O righteous
Father, although the world has not known Thee,
yet I have known Thee, and these have known that
Thou didst send Me; and I have made Thy name
known to them, and will make it known." Jesus
manifested the Abba-Fatherhood of God.

So the divinely given pattern for prayer is first
upward to God, not outward to humanity or inward to our needs. The thing we pray is that God's

"Abba-ness" will be known both in the Final Day and here in this needy world. "Abba, Father, let Your name be reverenced now and at the end of time—for all eternity!"

The Manward Aspect of the Foundational Petition

What does the upwardness of this petition mean to us? Does it simply focus upward, leaving our faces pointing toward the sky? No!

Martin Luther, in one of the questions of his Greater Catechism (*Grosser Katechismus*), said: "How is it [God's Name] hallowed amongst us?" Answer: "When our life and doctrine are truly Christian."

God's name is reverenced when we lead lives that reflect Him. We cannot truly pray, *"Hallowed be Thy name,"* without a dedication of ourselves. If we pray this without commitment, it is just idle talk.

Jesus is here the example *par excellence*. As the cross drew near, He prayed, "Father, glorify Thy name" (John 12:28), but He knew what this meant in terms of His own commitment. He gave His own life that the Father's name might be glorified.

How then do we, God's children, hallow His name in our own lives? There are at least four ways. First, negatively, we are careful not to profane God's name with our mouths. We avoid swearing or taking His name in vain. We speak of Him with great reverence. This is perhaps the least requiring aspect of hallowing His name.

Second, we begin with the positives: we reverence Him with acts of public and private worship. I personally consider the morning worship of my church to be the most important aspect of my life and ministry (apart from my personal devotion). Moreover, I do not consider my sermon to be the most important part of the service. What is the most important is the overall worship. Is God's name truly being lifted up? Are the hymns and Scriptures and prayers—and then the Word—lifting up His name? Most important: Is *my heart* worshiping? We are hallowing His name when we worship.

Then there is a third reason: We reverence God or hallow His name when our beliefs concerning Him are worthy of Him. We cannot hallow His name if we do not understand it. Specifically, in the Lord's Prayer we must understand His Abba-Fatherhood. The deeper our understanding, the more depth there is to our reverence.

This is the work of the Holy Spirit, of course; but it is also a work we are to set ourselves to— to understand the depth and wonder of saying, "Abba, Father" by the impulse of the Holy Spirit.

And fourthly, we hallow His name by living a life that displays that He is our Father. This has been the great application of this text for hundreds of years. It is the application set by Cyril, Cyprian, Augustine, Gregory of Nyssa, Martin Luther, John Calvin, and scores of others. Gregory offered this prayer in his exposition:

> May I become through thy help blameless, just and pious, may I abstain from every evil, speak the truth, and do justice. May I walk in the straight path, shining with temperance, adorned with incorruption, beautiful through wisdom and prudence. May I meditate upon the things that are above and despise what is earthly, showing the angelic way of life. . . . For a man can glorify God in no other way save by his virtue which bears witness that the Divine Power is the cause of his goodness.[3]

The leaders of the early church so strenuously stressed the quality of one's life because they lived in such a hostile environment. The only way they could spread Christianity was by living a life of such devotion and certitude that others would thirst for God the Father.

For us, hallowing God's name demands that we live lives that show we really do have a Heavenly Father. It demands that we display security and confidence in our Father when those without Christ are overcome in fear and despair. It demands that we radiate the self-esteem that comes from knowing we are loved by our "Dearest

Abba." It demands that we manifest the beautiful loyalty of a child toward its father in our devotion to God the Father.

But there is even more. We ought to model not just that we have a Father in heaven; we must also model God's loving Fatherliness to others. Psychologically speaking (ignoring God's obvious arrangement of my life), I think this is one of the reasons that I so wonderfully came to Christ at the age of twelve. My father had died when I was four, but when I was twelve, I met a pastor (the one who led me to Christ) who modeled God's Fatherhood to me. He was like God in that he was gentle and patient; like God because he was interested in me; like God because he was willing to be inconvenienced; like God because he cared about the smallest details in my life; like the Heavenly Father because he was concerned about the best for me and believed in me. Meeting a man like this after being without a father for eight years, I was inexorably drawn to *the* Father. And it is no wonder that when I came to Jesus at the age of twelve, "Dearest Father" became the refrain of my heart.

Luther was right. We best hallow God's name when our lives and our doctrine are truly Christian. When we pray, *"Our Father who art in heaven, hallowed be Thy name,"* we are dedicating ourselves to lead lives that hallow His name.

Let's not be *haolis*—those who fail to breathe

life into their prayers. Let's learn to take time to reflect on foundational realities of true prayer, that God is our Dear Father. Take time and breathe it in.

From this foundational awareness comes our foundational petition, "Hallowed be Thy name as Abba Father."

"God, may all historical differences and language vanish as all people bow to You as Father in the consummation of all things."

"And, God, may my life hallow Your name."

"May others see that I live as Your child."

"May others find me a caring parent like You."

"May my life be a continual invitation to Your family."

"Our Father who art in heaven, hallowed be Thy Name. Amen."

3

GOD'S KINGDOM

The second petition of the Lord's Prayer, *"Thy kingdom come,"* also extends the upward rush of the prayer begun in *"Hallowed be Thy name."* In fact, the Hebrew thought structure here demands that we understand both *"Thy kingdom come"* and *"Thy will be done"* as enlargements on *"Hallowed be Thy name."* The proper hallowing of God's name includes praying that His kingdom will come and His will be done. Prayer for the kingdom should be part of the pattern of our prayer life.

Over the years, conflicting interpretations have risen as to the meaning of *"Thy kingdom come."* Some have argued that it is a prayer for the Second Coming of Christ and that is all; that it has nothing to do with present life. Others have seen *"Thy kingdom come"* as a call to social action and nothing else—a mandate to bring in the kingdom now through good work. And there are those who have seen *"Thy kingdom come"* as spiritually fulfilled only in the salvation of souls.

Actually, the correct view contains elements of

all these views—as we will clearly see as we consider *"Thy kingdom come"* from the perspectives of the past, future, and present.

"Thy Kingdom Come" Recognizes the Past

The past requires only the briefest comment, which is this: praying *"Thy kingdom come"* does not suggest in the slightest way that God has not been or is not presently Sovereign King. "As He is already holy so He is already King, reigning in absolute sovereignty over both nature and history."[1] "The earth is the Lord's, and the fulness thereof; the world, and they that dwell therein" (Psalm 24:1, KJV).

Since God is already King, and His kingdom spans the entire universe, *"Thy kingdom come"* is a call for a new and unique manifestation of His kingdom. There is no doubt that the phrase must refer to the future.

"Thy Kingdom Come" Is for the Future

The time of the verb "come" refers to a decisive time in the future when the kingdom comes once and for all—an event which will happen only once.[2] This is the Second Advent of Christ, when He will return, judge the world, and set up His eternal kingdom. So strong is this idea in the Greek, *"Thy king-*

dom come," that Tertullian changed the order of the prayer, placing *"Thy will be done, on earth as it is in heaven" before "Thy kingdom come."* He reasoned that after the kingdom came, there would be no use praying, *"Thy will be done"*—everyone would be doing it!

Tertullian's reasoning was wrong, but he did accurately understand that *"Thy kingdom come"* is a prayer for the final kingdom when, under Christ's rule, our evil hearts will be pure; our lying and deceit, distrust and shame banished; our asylums and penitentiaries gone; and all conversation and literature and "business" carried on to the glory of God.

Men and women have longed for this since the Fall. We long for the time when there will be "righteousness and peace and joy in the Holy Spirit," as Paul describes the kingdom in Romans 14:17. Some may say that such thinking is "utopian"—and in the general sense of the word they may be right. But not utopian in the strict sense, because as the *Oxford English Dictionary* tells us, "utopia" comes from the Greek *ou,* "not," and *topos,* "a place," and means "not a place," and thus it signifies an impossible dream.

The coming advent of the kingdom of God is no impossibility. Let no one call it a utopia. It is as sure as any established fact of history. In it our dreams will come true!

The ultimate perfection of the kingdom can happen universally only in the eternal state—not in this world. Many Christians ignored this amidst the characteristic optimism of the nineteenth century, when it was commonly taught that the gospel would keep spreading until the kingdom would be ushered in. For example, toward the end of that century, a man named Sidney Gulick wrote a book entitled *The Growth of the Kingdom of God,* which was subsequently translated into Japanese in an attempt to persuade Japanese students to become Christians. The book's argument was that Christianity is inexorably spreading and will ultimately take over the world—so why not convert now? He reasoned:

> The Christian powers have increased the territory under their rule from about 7% of the surface of the world in 1600 to 82% in 1893, while the non-Christian powers have receded from about 93% to about 18% during the same period. At present the Protestant nations alone rule about twice as much territory as all the non-Christian nations combined.

He added,

> During the [first] ninety years of the religious history of the United States more persons have come under the direct influence of the Christian Church than during the first thousand years of Christianity in all lands combined.[3]

Needless to say, the Japanese weren't convinced of the argument. And, as has been pointed out, since the equation between the truth of religion and world domination has been so eloquently made, the Japanese attack on Pearl Harbor can be considered the logical result. Those who imagined that the kingdom could have been brought in by the preaching of the gospel neglected the teaching of the mystery parables of Matthew 13, such as "the sower" (vv. 4–23) and "the tares" (vv. 24–30), which demonstrate that the Church and its rule will be neither universal nor perfect.

What really put an end to such un-Biblical (though noble) dreams were the great wars—and sins—of the so-called "Christian nations." In 1945, Helmut Thielicke, the great theologian and preacher of the University of Hamburg, stood before his congregation in the choir of his church, which had been reduced to ruins by the air raids, and spoke these words:

> We must not think of it as a gradual Christianization of the world which will increasingly eliminate evil. Such dreams and delusions, which may have been plausible enough in more peaceful times, have vanished in the terrors of our man-made misery. The nineteenth century, which brought forth a number of these dreams and dreamers, strikes us today as being an age of unsuspecting children.[4]

Who can utter the word (progress) today without getting a flat taste in his mouth? Who can still believe today that we are developing toward a state in which the kingdom of God reigns in the world of nations, in culture, and in the life of the individual? The earth has been plowed too deep by the curse of war, the streams of blood and tears have swollen all too terribly, injustice and bestiality have become all too cruel and obvious for us to consider such dreams to be anything but bubbles and froth.[5]

Extreme pessimism? I do not think so. Actually, the sermon is one of remarkable optimism and encouragement, for in it Thielicke cries, "In the world of death, in this empire of ruins and shell-torn fields we pray: 'Thy kingdom come!' We pray it more fervently than ever."[6]

That is our ultimate hope. The future kingdom of God is coming. Then the angels will sing, "The kingdom of the world has become the kingdom of our Lord, and of His Christ; and He will reign forever and ever" (Revelation 11:15). His reign will be universal, as Jesus tells us: "And I say to you, that many shall come from east and west, and recline at table with Abraham, and Isaac, and Jacob, in the kingdom of heaven" (Matthew 8:11). Then all the world will own Him not only as sovereign, but as Abba Father. It will be the eternal refrain. It will be the world's golden age.

"Thy kingdom come" is to be part of the ground

and foundation of our prayers. We are to pray for the kingdom and eagerly await it with the same passion that Pastor Thielicke did as he stood in his worn boots in the rubble of 1945. "Maranatha," that is, "Come, O Lord!" is to be our cry. The next to the last verse in the Book of Revelation says the same: "Amen. Come, Lord Jesus" (22:20). It is a big prayer. Are we big enough to pray it?

Having only half discussed the subject, it might be easy to conclude that *"Thy kingdom come"* promotes a laissez-faire, other-worldly attitude. No conclusion could be more mistaken.

"Thy Kingdom Come" Is for the Present

We must understand that when Jesus came, He brought the kingdom of God in His person. When He began His public ministry, the very first words from His mouth after reading from Isaiah were, "Repent, for the kingdom of heaven is at hand" (Matthew 4:17). Later He said of Himself, "The kingdom of God is in your midst" (Luke 17:21). We can say that Jesus *was* the kingdom because He was the only person who ever fully accepted and fully carried out God's will.

Jesus' passion was the kingdom. It was the major theme of His preaching. The word "kingdom" occurs forty-nine times in Matthew, sixteen in Mark, and thirty-eight in Luke—103 times! Before the cross He said, "I must preach the kingdom of God to the other cities also, for I was sent for this purpose" (Luke 4:43). After the Resurrection it was still His message as He appeared to His disciples "over a period of forty days, . . . speaking of the things concerning the kingdom of God" (Acts 1:3). Preaching the kingdom was His consuming passion.

How did He bring the kingdom? Primarily by bringing men and women into obedience to the Father's will. This is the meaning of *"Thy kingdom come"* in its context, because the immediately following and parallel words are, *"Thy will be done on earth as it is in heaven."* Those who are in God's kingdom strive to do God's will—in fact, they do it.

When we see this, it is impossible to leave the kingdom out there. Rather, it becomes a very personal thing for several reasons. First, although my will wants to go its own way, being in the kingdom means my will is redirected to God's will. This is what repentance means. Jesus was always saying, "Repent, for the kingdom of God is at hand" (Mark 1:14, 15 and Matthew 4:17). Being a Christian, a member of the kingdom, means that increasingly what God wants becomes what we want. To pray *"Thy kingdom come"* is to repent.

Second, it demands commitment. Jesus was very emphatic when He said, "No one after putting his hand to the plow and looking back, is fit for the kingdom of God" (Luke 9:62). The kingdom of God is for those who have decided to follow Him and who do not keep longingly looking back. To pray *"Thy kingdom come"* is to commit ourselves.

Third, the kingdom is, therefore, to be pursued above all else. Jesus again gave the authoritative word: "But seek first His kingdom, and His righteousness; and all these things shall be added to you" (Matthew 6:33).

Before all else, we are to seek the kingdom in obedience to Him. This destroys any idea of easygoing, do-nothing, armchair Christianity. We cannot pray the Lord's Prayer with folded hands. To pray *"Thy kingdom come"* is to pursue it.

Fourth, the kingdom of God is for those who have a profound dependence upon God. We cannot overquote Jesus' words, "Blessed are the poor in spirit [those who realize that they have nothing within themselves to commend them to God], for theirs [theirs alone!] is the kingdom of heaven" (Matthew 5:3). No one else has the kingdom except those who have come to the end of themselves.

In these four points I have sketched something of the depth of commitment that praying *"Thy kingdom come"* demands of us. This commitment then produces a life which makes a difference in society and the world. Kingdom power is brought to bear in our most intimate relationships. Lives are influenced for Christ—some are changed. We make a difference in our schools. The ethics of those who rule our city are touched by the kingdom. Sometimes whole societies are elevated.

To pray *"Thy kingdom come"* is to reject the corrupt social structures of our day and strive for a redeemed community. It is to work toward transforming our community and society. To pray *"Thy kingdom come"* is a commitment to live out the Beatitudes and the ethics of the Sermon on the Mount.

That will be kingdom living now: a poverty of spirit, a mourning over the sins of the world, a requisite humility that springs out of those things, a hungering and thirsting after righteousness, a merciful, forgiving spirit—merciful in that we also get involved in society and life—a singleness and commitment to God, and possibly persecution. That will affect society.

Our vision for society, our ideal, is the kingdom; and that is what we strive for. To be sure, we will never succeed in establishing the final *perfect* kingdom as was supposed by some of our forebears. The great wars have painfully taught us that. However, kingdom living now has made and does make a difference in the world. Virtually all the great social reforms have their roots in kingdom living.

The abolition of slavery came through kingdom living and one William Wilberforce. Prison reform came from the kingdom living of Elizabeth Fry. And the great advances in compassion and medical care through nursing came through Florence Nightingale. We do make a difference when we pray truly *"Thy kingdom come."*

An even more contemporary example of a great Christian social reformer is Jonathan Blanchard, founder of Wheaton College. Blanchard understood the kingdom of God as "Christ ruling in and over rational creatures who are obeying Him freely and from choice, under no constraint but that of love."

Thus Blanchard opposed those who emphasized that such a kingdom is not to be sought in this world, insisting that though "this kingdom is not *of* this world, it is *in* it." Carrying this affirmation to its logical conclusion, Blanchard warned against both those who "locate Christ's kingdom in the future to the neglect of the present" and those who "seek to construct a local heaven upon earth . . . thus shutting out the influences and motives of eternity."

Prompted by this vision and compelled by obedience to Christ's command to "seek ye first the kingdom of God," Blanchard was propelled into a life of reform that climaxed in the founding of Wheaton College. His life was so dominated by reform that upon his death, the *Political Dissenter* commented that "in the death of Dr. Jonathan Blanchard, American reformers have lost one of their foremost leaders. No more fearless voice ever rang out on the platform, or from the pulpit. No keener or more valiant pen has been wielded against popular wrongs, and in defense of unpopular truth."[7]

When we pray *"Thy kingdom come,"* we pray for three things. First, we pray for the final and ultimate establishment of His kingdom. We pray for the day when all creation will freely call Him "Dearest Father"—"Abba." We pray for the day when all will be "righteousness and peace and joy in the Holy Spirit" (Romans 14:17).

Here there is an almost martial, triumphant ring to *"Thy kingdom come."* "Maranatha!" "Come, O Lord!"

Second, we pray *"Thy kingdom come,"* asking that we will be obedient to His will in this world. This is no prayer for people who want to stay the way they are. As we pray this, we hand ourselves over to the grace of God so that He may do with us as He pleases. *"Thy kingdom come* in my life. Use me for Your kingdom."

Third, *"Thy kingdom come"* is also a prayer that God's rule may come to others through us. It is a prayer for Christ to work His revolutionary power in a fallen world. "Thy kingdom come in my family, my job, my city, my nation."

It is a big prayer which demands a big God and, when truly prayed, makes for a big life. Are our lives big enough to pray, *"Thy kingdom come"?*

There is one final thing. The Scriptures picture

the kingdom as a feast with people coming from east and west to recline together at table (Matthew 8:11). Certainly we look forward to the marriage feast of the Lamb when we will sit down with Christ, and He will be our everything. Such is our expectation when the kingdom comes!

Pray, then, in this way: *"Our Father who art in heaven, Hallowed be Thy name. Thy kingdom come. Amen."*

4

GOD'S
WILL

"T hy will be done, on earth as it is in heaven" is the third and final Godward request of the Lord's model prayer. With this phrase, we come to what is surely the most abused of the Prayer's six petitions.

As we know, the Lord's Prayer is mindlessly repeated thousands of times every Lord's Day, as well as other times. From what I have seen over the years, Hollywood thinks that it makes a perfect conclusion to a war movie. You know the story line: the "Terrible Ten" have been killing the enemy with ferocious joy and cohabiting with the local girls. The only time God has been mentioned is in their curses. But now the enemy has them encircled, their ammo is gone, and they need to do something religious—so they begin to pray, *"Our Father . . .,"* because deep down inside they are really "good guys."

It's true that the whole of the Lord's Prayer is

misused, both in and outside the church, but the abuse of this line is perhaps even deeper. This particular line is prayed by people who have never even had the intention of doing God's will. Think of the words! "Thy will be done, *on earth as it is in heaven.*" What a solemn thing to pray.

Luther called it a "fearful prayer," for if some people realized what they were praying, their words would stick in their throats. It is of the greatest importance that we understand what we are praying, and pray it with the utmost sincerity.

It is also important because submitting our will to God is one of our greatest needs. None of us finds it easy. We all like to be the "captains of our souls"—and often we retake the command we once humbly and wisely relinquished.

Some people have more difficulty than others with God's will because they never received consistent guidance from anyone as children. Because of this, they are at a disadvantage, though they dearly want to conform to God's will. It's not easy for anyone. But for some it is even harder.

But Jesus' words are for *all* of us. Jesus tells us here that the ideal prayer should contain a section in which we bow before God saying, "Let Your will be done right here, just as it is in heaven itself." Do we truly pray this? And if we do, what do we mean? There is not a person who will not benefit by facing these questions.

Jesus Calls Us to Pray
for the World's Obedience

What is Jesus asking us to pray for when He tells us to pray, *"Thy will be done, on earth as it is in heaven"?* The answer is, first of all, that Jesus is calling us to pray for the world's obedience.

The call is two-fold. First, we pray for the universal obedience that will come at the end of history. In the final kingdom there will be no necessity for guidelines about retaliation, hate, lust, or hypocrisy because there will be no hatred or hypocrisy. God's will will prevail everywhere. *"Thy will be done, on earth as it is in heaven"* focuses us on this final inevitable event and fills us with hope in this troubled world.

Secondly, the prayer calls for God's will to be done right now in present history. To those who question how this is possible, Jesus answers with His life. Early in His ministry, Jesus told His disciples, "My food is to do *the will* of Him who sent Me" (John 4:34). This food is not an extra or a dessert by which we top our lives with a bit of religion. Our food, the main course of our lives, is His will.

Just as I live by my daily bread, just as my heart and my eyes and my whole body are driven toward food by the spontaneous urge of hunger, so I live by the will of the Father, so I am driven to him and linked to him with every fiber of my being.[1]

Later Jesus again said, "I do not seek my own will, but the will of Him who sent Me" (John 5:30). And again, "For I have come down from heaven, not to do My own will, but the will of Him who sent Me" (John 6:38). And finally in Gethsemane, in the bloody sweat, He cried to His Father, "Abba! Father! All things are possible for Thee; remove this cup from Me; yet not what I will, but what Thou wilt" (Mark 14:36).

Every earthly beat of Christ's heart was given to the will of the Father. In Jesus, God's will was perfectly lived in human history.

And it is possible for men and women, despite their imperfections, to live lives that work out God's will in history. We are to pray that this happens so that not only His salvation, but also His ethical will is done—that righteousness and justice are brought to bear in this fallen world.

"Thy will be done, on earth as it is in heaven" is a massive prayer, for it encompasses both history and posthistory. It is stridently upward. "Father, *Thy* will (no other will) be done just as it is in heaven." It is a *command* (aorist passive imperative), and as such demands passionate expression. "Father, *let* Your will be done on earth as it is in heaven."

Have we ever prayed this with force? The text

warrants it, even invites it. Why not do it with all your heart?

Jesus Calls Us to Pray for Our Own Individual Obedience

"Thy will be done, on earth"—in me!—*"as it is in heaven."* This phrase is an invitation for God to conquer us—and that is why it can be so frightening. When we pray this prayer, we are asking God to do what is necessary to make His will prevail in our lives. It is a prayer that often invites trouble, as God then comes in gracious, kind violence to root out all impediments to obedience.

To pray this prayer may terrify us, but it will also deliver us from ourselves. It can truly be said that we have not learned to pray at all until every request in our prayers is made subject to this one. *"Thy will be done"* is the petition that determines the authenticity of the other upward petitions, for if we do not mean it, we cannot really pray, *"Hallowed be Thy name"* or *"Thy kingdom come."*

Genuinely praying *"Thy will be done"* is fundamental to all true prayer.

What is our obedience to be like? The key is found in the second half of the petition, *" . . . as it is in heaven."* Not only is God's will to be done by us, but we are to do it just as those in heaven are doing it at this moment. How is it done in heaven?

Here I think the tone of voice with which we say *"Thy will be done"* will serve as a good illustration. It is possible to say *"Thy will be done"* in a tone of bitter resentment.

Julian was the Roman Emperor who tried to put the clock back. He tried to reverse the decision of Constantine that Christianity should be the religion of the Empire, and he tried to reintroduce the worship and the service and the ceremonies of the ancient gods. In the end he was mortally wounded in battle in the east. The historians tell how, when he lay bleeding to death, he took a handful of his blood and tossed it in the air, saying: "You have conquered, O man of Galilee!"[2]

We can say *"Thy will be done"* through angry, clenched lips. That is not heaven's tone. It is also possible to say *"Thy will be done"* in a funereal tone of resignation and defeat, which goes best with the smell of flowers. "God, I wanted things my way, but they are not turning out. . . . So I shall turn them over to You, for Your competitive will has more power than mine and will probably have its way anyhow. So teach me not to grumble too much about how things are going against me."[3]

" *'Thy will be done'*—anyway."

Or we can say *"Thy will be done"* with a note of cheer and buoyancy. We know that this is the way it is in heaven. The glorified saints and angels find their greatest joy in doing His will. They probably wrestle each other for the privilege. And they probably do it with singing, if the heavenly vignettes from the Book of Revelation tell us anything.

So when we pray this third petition of the Lord's Prayer, we are praying for two things. First, that we ourselves will live in profound obedience, that His will may be the supreme desire of our lives; and second, that our obedience may be *"as it is in heaven"*—joyous, bounding, and enthusiastic. This is what we all want.

How, then, can we attain to it? Besides the obvious, which is to pray that His will be done and then consciously submit to it, there are some things to keep in mind. Foremost is the fact that this entire prayer is controlled by the word *"Father."* Here *"Thy will"* is God's will—the will of One we call "Abba"—"Dearest Father." You and I are asked to do the will of our Father whose love is measured by the cross of Jesus Christ. The fact that His will issues from such love ought to be the greatest encouragement to do it.

My father-love, as imperfect as it is, always desires the best for my children. All healthy parents dream, and even scheme, to secure a happy and prosperous future for their children. When my wife and I go out for our traditional Monday breakfast, most of our conversation centers on our children. We do talk about other things, but our beginning conversation is about our children.

We talk about the pressure that one child is under, the good week of another, what we think is best for each child, what we need to pray about for them, and we make lists of things they need.

The mental focus of a caring parent is terrific. If one of mine is having a difficult time, it affects me. I can have had the greatest weekend, Sunday can have been terrific; but if one of my children is down, my day is heavy. The unalterable reality is that my father-love and father-will for them (imperfect as it is) has only the best in mind for them.

Focusing this back on our text, to pray *"Thy will be done"* is to pray that the perfect, loving, caring will of our Heavenly Father be done in our lives. It is to pray that what is "good and acceptable and perfect" (Romans 12:2) be done in our lives. This is what we need to keep in mind as we attempt to grow in obedience to God's will. What foolishness it is to resist His loving will. It is resisting the best. It is resisting love.

Another thing to keep in mind as we strive to grow in obedience is that in order to do God's will, we need to know God's will. Thus, when we truly pray *"Thy will be done,"* there must be a corresponding commitment to learning all we can about it.

This means the continual study of the Scriptures, which are the main revelatory agency of His will. The church makes bold claims for this book (claims the book makes for itself). It believes it is infallible. But the ignorance of the people in the church contradicts these spoken beliefs. To truly pray *"Thy will be done"* is to commit ourselves to knowing God's will as it is revealed in His Word—and then to do it.

The last thing we must keep in mind if we want to grow in obedience is this: in His will is our greatest joy. Elisabeth Elliot once stayed in the farmhouse of a Welsh shepherd and his family high in the mountains of North Wales. She stood watching one misty summer morning as the shepherd on horseback herded the sheep with the aid of his champion Scottish collie named Mack. In her own words:

Mack . . . was in his glory. He came of a long line of working dogs, and he had sheep in his blood. This was what he was made for; this was what he had been trained to do. It was a marvelous thing to see him circling to the right, circling to the left, barking, crouching, racing along, herding a stray sheep here, nipping at a stubborn one there, his eyes always glued to the sheep, his ears listening for the tiny metal whistle from his master that I couldn't hear.[4]

That day, Mack assisted his master, who had arranged to dip his struggling sheep. Mack was beautiful. As the sheep would attempt to escape the tub, he would snarl and snap at their faces to force them back in. Mack's every move in the pen or out in the pasture was perfect. He seemed as good as the shepherd himself. Amazed, Elisabeth Elliot asked the shepherd's wife if the sheep had any idea what was happening. "Not a clue!" was the answer. "And how about Mack?" The answer, she says, was unforgettable. "The dog doesn't understand the pattern—only obedience." And then Elisabeth Elliot reflected:

> I saw two creatures who were in the fullest sense "in their glory." A man who had given his life to sheep, who loved them and loved his dog. And a dog whose trust in that man was absolute, whose obedience was instant and unconditional, and whose very meat and drink was to do the will of his master. "I delight to do thy will," was what Mack said, "Yea, thy law is within my heart."
> To experience the glory of God's will for us means absolute trust. It means the will to do His will, and means joy.[5]

Elisabeth Elliot is right. Never are we greater —never do we know greater joy—than when we do His will.

We have an advantage over Mack the collie, for we can understand something of the pattern and something of our Shepherd. He is the Creator, the One who set the stars in their trajectories. He is the God who, in the Person of Jesus Christ, created the universe with His own hands and then allowed those hands to be nailed to the cross. And we can trust Him.

This is our greatest glory—to pray and live the prayer, *"Thy will be done, on earth as it is in heaven."* What joy and glory comes from obedience, absolute and unconditional. People only are what they ought to be whose wills are bound to God's.

To glibly parrot this prayer does nothing. To pray it sincerely has revolutionary implications. When we truly pray *"Thy will be done, on earth as it is in heaven,"* we pray for the world's obedience. We pray for the final day when all will bow, and we also pray for the here and now. We pray for that which is surely coming, and unite ourselves with future victory even while we reside in a disobedient world.

We also pray for our own obedience. *"Thy will be done"* means, "God, conquer me!" *"On earth as it is in heaven"* means that I want my submission to be like the submission in heaven— eager, cheerful, buoyant.

And we want to do it! Remember: God is our "Dearest Father," and in His will is the greatest glory and joy.

Why not pray the Lord's Prayer now with all your heart: *"Thy will be done, on earth as it is in heaven."* We either line ourselves up with the Son of God and say to the Father, *"Thy will be done,"* or we give in to the principle which controls the rest of the world and say, "My will be done."

Obedience to God is action, an act of the will. We must put ourselves in His hands, choose to give ourselves.

"I urge you therefore, brethren, by the mercies of God, to present your bodies a living and holy sacrifice, acceptable to God, which is your spiritual service of worship" (Romans 12:1).

"Pray then, in this way: 'Our Father, who art in heaven, Hallowed be Thy name. Thy kingdom come. Thy will be done, On earth as it is in heaven'" (Matthew 6:9, 10).

5

OUR
BREAD

When Jesus responded to the disciples' request that He teach them how to pray, He gave them the most perfect and comprehensive outline ever conceived in what we have come to call "the Lord's Prayer." As we have often noted thus far, the prayer consists of six petitions (or requests). The first three have to do with God's glory and are distinguished by the word "Thy": *"Thy name," "Thy kingdom,"* and *"Thy will."* The second three, which we come to now, have to do with human well-being and are distinguished by the word *"us:" "give us," "forgive us,"* and *"lead us."*

The extraordinary comprehensiveness of these six petitions caused Helmut Thielicke to remark that they are like the colors of the spectrum into which light divides when it shines through a prism. The whole light of life is captured in the rainbow of the petitions. No one can say that the Prayer does not take into account his or her need.

Great things, small things, spiritual things and material things, inward things and outward things—there is nothing that is not included in this prayer.[1]

In these last three petitions, then, we turn from praying for God's glory to praying for our needs. Through them, we can learn how to begin praying for ourselves.

How can we properly pray for ourselves? The answer is very helpful, because it does away with some pious presuppositions which are commonly held, and frees us to pray naturally, from the heart.

The initial petition (in verse 11) seems simple enough: *"Give us this day our daily bread."* In English, the phrase contains only seven words—and six of them are monosyllables. There ought not be any trouble here, we think. Little do we know! The only two-syllable word, *"daily,"* has been the source of a great controversy (which, by the way, has nothing to do with its being two syllables in English).

The problem stems from the fact that this is the *only* occurrence of the word in all of Greek literature. You can search all the Greek classics from Homer to the New Testament and you will find no such word, except here. It was found once in a nonliterary source: on a papyrus fragment containing a grocery list, where it *seemed* to indicate the necessities of the day. But this single occurrence is inconclusive.

Today, scholars tell us that the word can mean either "today's bread" or "tomorrow's bread," bread for tomorrow. But according to them, there is little doubt that it means "bread for tomorrow." So, the Lord's Prayer should literally read, "Give us this day our bread for tomorrow," as the margins of the RSV and NEB have it.[2]

What does this do to the meaning of the Lord's Prayer? In the basic sense, very little, because if the prayer is prayed in the morning, it will be a prayer for the needs of the day. And if it is prayed in the evening, it will be a prayer for the needs of the next day. So the primary sense is still the same, because "give us today tomorrow's bread" is a prayer for God to meet our daily physical needs.

However, at the same time, praying for tomorrow's bread implicitly requests that God meet our needs with the bread of the ultimate tomorrow—the bread of eternity—as we shall see.

We Are to Pray
for Our Physical Needs

So let us begin first with the basic meaning of, *"Give us this day our daily* (or tomorrow's) *bread,"* which is that we are to pray for our physical needs.

It is fascinating that the early Church Fathers rejected this plain meaning and spiritualized the bread to mean the bread of Communion. Jerome called it, in his translation of the Bible, *Panem nostrum supersubstantialem*, or supersubstantial bread—bread that is more than physical. He did this mainly because, to him, it just did not seem right after the first three upward petitions for God's glory, to immediately switch to something so crass as asking for our material well-being. To Jerome, the first part of the prayer was so completely selfless, that then to pray for bread seemed inappropriately selfish, narrow, and materialistic.

However, despite all the rationalizing and theologizing, *"our daily bread"* means exactly what it says. We are to pray for our physical provision. In fact, that is the first thing God tells us to pray for when we pray for ourselves.

That we should pray for our material well-being of course demands some thoughtful application. First, *"Give us this day our daily bread"* is not carte blanche to pray for everything in the Sears catalog (or the Neiman Marcus catalog—if that is what you read). I once sat with a group of ministers and listened to another minister—who was later indicted by a grand jury for fraud and convicted—tell us that if we wanted Cadillacs or large wardrobes, it was God's will for us. His rationale was that Psalm 37:4 says, "Delight yourself in the Lord; and He will give you the desires of your heart." Therefore, he concluded, if we ministers were delighting ourselves in the Lord, and at the same time our hearts desired Cadillacs and Gucci shoes and Tiffany, it must be God's will and we should believe God for them. End of rationalization.

No Scripture teaches such foolishness, and especially not the Lord's Prayer. The Lord's Prayer calls us to pray for *"bread"*—that is, the necessities of life—those things that are essential for the life and health and well-being of ourselves and our families. We are to pray for *bread,* not dessert.

Second, *"Give us this day our daily bread"* is an invitation to come to God with those things others might call small. One of the precious realities of our Christian walk is that God cares for the simple, ordinary, day-to-day things of life.

Jesus taught us that the so-called "little things" are important to God. He took the babies in His arms and loved them and blessed them when His disciples would have sent them away. He bestowed His special love upon the seemingly worthless existences of those who were in society's eyes the least of all people: the lepers, the lame, and the mentally ill.

God is pleased to occupy Himself with the small things of human existence. God cares whether His people are warm, well-fed, and well-housed.

And besides, these things are not so little when we are without them! And when these "little things" are taken away, the big things don't seem so big. "A Beethoven symphony, which for many people may come close to being ranked as a divine revelation, sounds quite different if we listen to it when we are shivering with cold. And a visit to an art gallery is even less edifying . . . when we undertake it on an empty stomach."[3] If you are freezing, a warm sweater has higher priority than a volume of C. S. Lewis poems.

The abiding, blessed truth of our text is that God wants us to bring our everyday needs to Him, even if they appear trivial. He doesn't demand that we approach Him only when we have raised ourselves to some kind of spiritual elevation above the everyday things of life. He comes to meet us where we are, and therein lies His greatness. When we come to Him with our "little things," we do Him great honor.

Which leads to the third point: in commanding us to pray *"Give us this day our daily bread,"* God is fostering in us a daily dependence upon Himself. How this flies against the times in which we live! There is no other line in the Lord's Prayer which so sharply challenges the direction of today's world. The average person wants to compound his or her security and thus his or her independence.

To be sure, there is nothing wrong with planning for future rainy days, but it is wrong to make total independence our consuming goal—our preoccupation. The point is, whether we are rich or poor, God wants us to depend upon Him daily. He wants us all to pray for our daily needs—and He wants us to daily thank Him, saying, *"Give us this day our daily bread."*

Lastly, God wants to build a mutuality between us and our brothers and sisters through this prayer. He commands us to pray, "give us," not "give me." Every time we pray this prayer with our heart and mind, we are affirming our solidarity with our brothers and sisters. When we pray "Give *us* this day *our* daily bread," we are making an implicit commitment to help provide bread for needy friends. The prayer is a stretching, broadening petition. We commit ourselves to be part of God's answer.

God wants to free us up. We don't have to hike ourselves up to some lofty spiritual plain, above the material and mundane, before we make our requests. We aren't instructed to bring only the big things to God. We are to bring our small requests— our requests for the bread we need, a coat, shoes, a car, books, a vacation, exercise, a bicycle, groceries.

. . . he whose eye encompasses in its boundless reach the first day of creation and the last hour of judgment, reflecting all the eternities; he whose outstretched arm enfolds the oceans, islands, and continents, because all authority in heaven and earth has been given to him, he occupies himself with the trivialities of humankind.[4]

God cares about our everyday needs. Why not resolve right now to take them to Him? If we have never understood our privilege to take the small things to Him, and we now understand it and exercise it, this can be one of the great days of our life.

We Are to Pray
for Our Spiritual Bread

Having seen that the basic, primary meaning of this fourth petition is for physical bread, we now turn to its secondary meaning, which is the spiritual bread characteristic of the eternal state. I believe there is this dual interpretation for several reasons.

First, the petition actually reads, "Give us this day our bread for tomorrow," and so it points to the special bread of the future state.

Second, the three preceding petitions of the prayer all refer ultimately to the final eternal state, when God's name is once and for all hallowed, His kingdom comes, and His will is perpetually done. Therefore, it follows that the bread of tomorrow is also eternal.

Third, Jesus used only one symbol to describe the eternal state for believers, and He used it many times. It is the picture of a great, joyous feast.[5] Surely this is where the "bread of heaven" will be served. Thus, in three ways we see that when Jesus bids us to pray for the bread of tomorrow, He is bidding us to pray for the bread of eternity today.

Here in the Lord's Prayer, the Lord Jesus tells us, His children, that through prayer we can stretch out our hands and grasp the glorious bread of eternity and feast upon it. The ultimate bread is, of course, Christ. Jesus Himself said,

> "I am the living bread that came down out of heaven; if any one eats of this bread, he shall live forever; and the bread also which I shall give for the life of the world is My flesh" (John 6:51).

And we say back in response:

> By Thee the souls of men are fed
>   With gifts of grace supernal:
> Thou, who dost give us earthly bread,
>   Give us the bread eternal.

Jesus never disappoints. He always gives this bread to those who ask. I once read of a woman who, in the Christmas rush, purchased fifty greeting cards without looking at the message inside. She signed and addressed all but a few, and then dropped them in the mailbox, still without taking the time to see what they said. However, a few days later when things had slowed down, she picked one up and this is what she read—to her great embarrassment:

> This card is just to say
> A little gift is on the way.

Needless to say, there were some fifty disappointed families who never received their presents. Jesus isn't like that. He never disappoints. He calls us to pray for the "bread of tomorrow," and He gives us Himself.

When we pray *"Give us this day our daily bread,"* we pray for two breads. We pray for physical bread. We are to ask our Father to meet our daily needs. In doing so we glorify Him, and we grow in our dependence upon Him—just as He wishes. We need to bring our daily needs to Him.

We also pray for spiritual bread. Literally, we ask for the "bread of tomorrow."

When we take Communion, the table before us symbolizes both our physical bread and the spiritual bread of the kingdom. The Lord's Supper is a foretaste for us, the followers of Jesus, of the coming kingdom in all its fullness, when we shall sit down with one another with Jesus at the head of the table. The bread we eat at the Communion table is real bread. It tastes of the past, when our blessed Lord's body was broken for us on the cross. It also tastes of tomorrow.

Lord, "give us this day the bread of tomorrow. Amen."

6

OUR
FORGIVENESS

Robert Louis Stevenson in his *Picturesque Notes of Edinburgh* tells the story of two unmarried sisters who shared a single room. As people are apt to do who live in close quarters, the sisters had a falling out, which Stevenson says was "on some point of controversial divinity"—in other words, they disagreed over some aspect of theology. The controversy was so bitter that they never spoke again (ever!) to one another. There were no words, either kind or spiteful. Just silence.

You would think that they would have separated, but nothing of the sort. Possibly it was because of lack of means, or of the innate Scottish fear of scandal, that they continued to keep house together in the single room. A chalk-line was drawn across the floor which separated their two domains. It divided the doorway and the fireplace, so that each could go in and out and do her cooking without stepping into the territory of the other.

So for years they coexisted in hateful silence. Their meals, their baths, their family visitors were exposed to the other's unfriendly silence. And at night, each went to bed listening to the heavy breathing of her enemy.[1] Thus, the two sisters (ostensibly daughters of the church!) continued the rest of their miserable lives.

No doubt when they attended church they were compelled often to "say" the Lord's Prayer. They obviously never truly prayed it—for it would have meant their reconciliation. The spiritual mutuality which the first three upward petitions enjoin as they begin with the words, *"Our Father,"* would have called them up short. How could they truly pray *"Our Father"* and remain estranged? And if that didn't do it, perhaps the first horizontal petition, "Give *us* this day *our* daily bread," would have reconciled them.

And if neither of these worked, there would be the next petition, *"Forgive us our debts, as we forgive our debtors." "Forgive us . . . as we forgive."* There is no way they could have remained bitter and unforgiving and *truly* prayed these words.

This text, *"Forgive us our debts, as we forgive our debtors,"* is eminently remedial. Seriously prayed, it can be the healing salve for a fractured spiritual life and broken human relationships. It is our Lord's second great instruction on how we ought to pray concerning ourselves. This petition (Matthew 6:12) is an explicit prayer for forgiveness, *"Forgive us our debts,"* and it is also an implicit prayer for a forgiving spirit: " . . . *as we forgive our debtors."*

So Jesus is telling us that ideal prayer contains both a request for personal forgiveness and a request for a forgiving spirit. Let us begin with the *second* clause.

A Prayer for a Forgiving Spirit

St. Augustine called this request "the terrible petition," because he realized that if we pray "Forgive us our debts *as we forgive our debtors*" with an unforgiving heart, we are actually asking God *not* to forgive us. We see this clearly if we substitute for the word "debt" the word "sin," which is its intrinsic meaning. Then the petition reads, "Forgive us our sins as we forgive those who sin against us."

Jesus does not want anyone to misunderstand, so He states it categorically in verses 14 and 15: "For if you forgive men for their transgressions, your heavenly Father will also forgive you. But if you do not forgive men, then your Father will not forgive your transgressions."

Startling words! Yet shocking as Jesus' statement is, it was really nothing new, but was common to Jewish understanding. The author of the apocryphal book Ecclesiasticus, the Wisdom of Jesus the Son of Sirach, says this: "Forgive your neighbor the wrong he has done, and then your sins will be pardoned when you pray."

Then, to drive home his statement, the writer of Ecclesiasticus asks three questions.

First, "Does a man harbor anger against another and yet seek for healing from the Lord?" The unspoken answer is "Absurd!"

Second, "Does he have no mercy toward a man like himself, and yet pray for his own sins?" That can't be.

Third, "If he himself, being flesh, maintain wrath, who will make expiation for his sins?"[2]

Thus we see that Jesus' words were in accordance with the ancient understanding of God's people.

The New Testament fully corroborates itself on this teaching several times. Matthew 5:7 says, "Blessed are the merciful, for they shall receive mercy." A merciless, unforgiving heart will receive neither forgiveness nor mercy. James 2:13 says the same: "For judgment will be merciless to one who has shown no mercy." And Jesus' powerful parable of the man who was forgiven ten thousand talents by his lord, but refused to forgive his own slave a hundred-denarii debt, ends with this terrifying warning:

"Then summoning him, his lord said to him, 'You wicked slave, I forgave you all that debt because you entreated me. Should you not also have had mercy on your fellow-slave, even as I had mercy on you?' And his lord, moved with anger, handed him over to the torturers until he should repay all that was owed him. So shall My heavenly Father also do to you, if each of you does not forgive his brother from your heart" (Matthew 18:32-35).

So, we are in no doubt that Jesus means exactly what He says: "If you do not forgive men, then your Father will not forgive your transgressions" (Matthew 6:15).

It was just such an awareness that occasioned one of John Wesley's famous statements. Wesley was serving as a missionary to the Colonies and was having a terrible time with General Oglethorpe, who was noted for his pride and unbending nature. In a particularly prideful moment Oglethorpe said, "I never forgive." To which Wesley replied, "Then I hope, sir, you never sin."

Wesley knew that if we pride ourselves on never forgetting a wrong, if we make our unforgiving spirit a virtue, we cannot *be* forgiven. Thomas Watson, the great Puritan, said, "A man can as well go to hell for not forgiving as for not believing."[3]

Charles Spurgeon agreed: "Unless you have forgiven others, you read your own death-warrant when you repeat the Lord's Prayer."[4] And in our day, C. S. Lewis says:

No part of his teaching is clearer: and there are no exceptions to it. He doesn't say that we are to forgive other people's sins providing they are not too frightful, or provided there are extenuating circumstances, or anything of that sort. We are to forgive them all, however spiteful, however mean, however often they are repeated. If we don't, we shall be forgiven none of our own.[5]

It is a fact: sometimes our unforgiving hearts make our prayers die on our lips. The Lord's Prayer can actually become to us a self-inflicted curse—a prayer of doom instead of blessing! What we are really praying may actually sound something like this: "I beseech you, Lord, deal with me as I deal with my neighbor. He has been ungrateful to me (though not a one hundredth as ungrateful as I have been to You), yet I cannot overlook his ingratitude. Deal with me, Lord, as I do him."

Or this: "I remember and treasure up every little incident in which she mistreats me. Deal with me, Lord, I pray, as I deal with her."

Or this: "The first opportunity I get to pay him back will bring me such joy. Deal with me, Lord, as I deal with him!"

Let us extend the principle even further. If we will not forgive, we are not Christians! I realize that this is a frightening thing to say—that we cannot be forgiven unless we have a forgiving spirit. But it is true, for when God's grace comes into our hearts, it makes us forgiving. We demonstrate whether we have been forgiven by whether or not we will forgive. So the bottom line is this: if I refuse to forgive, there can be only one reason, and that is that I have never understood the grace of Christ. I am outside grace, and I am unforgiven.

These are hard words, but they are graciously hard. They are for religious people who can state all the answers, who attend church, who lead an outwardly moral life, perhaps a life of negation (they do not do a lot of things), but who hold a death grip on their grudges. They will not forgive their relatives for some infraction; they have no desire to pardon their former business associates, no matter what they do; they nourish hatred, cherish animosities, revel in malice. Such people had better take an honest inventory of their lives and see if they really know Jesus.

Here I think a few words of qualification are in order. We are not referring to those who find that bitterness and hatreds recur even though they have forgiven the offender. The fact that we have forgiven and continue to forgive is a sign of grace. We are not talking about people who are struggling with forgiveness. We are referring to those who have *no desire* to forgive. These are the ones in soul danger. There also may be some who have been recently offended and are still in emotional shock, so that they haven't been able to properly respond in forgiveness.

The point is: if we are Christians, we can and will ultimately forgive.

The question for us is this, is *"Forgive us our debts as we forgive our debtors"* a curse upon us or a blessing? Are our most precious possessions our grudges? Do we pride ourselves on the fact that we never forgive? If so, the chances are very good that we are not believers.

How good of God to put it this way. It requires no elaborate reasoning process to determine where we are—no special knowledge—no "club words." All it requires is honesty. Does the state of your heart as to forgiveness indicate grace or not?

This fifth petition of the Lord's Prayer not only helps us to understand whether we are believers or not; but, if we are believers, it also helps us to monitor our spiritual health. We all have the unhealthy tendency to be more conscious of the wrongs done to us than the wrongs we have done to others. There is something within us which makes us tend to minimize the wrongs we have done to others. When others are hurt, we credit it to their oversensitive feelings. But when we are wronged, we tend to exaggerate our own hurt and the evil of the offender.

Lewis says of this:

> In our own case we accept excuses too easily, in other people's we do not accept them easily enough. As regards my own sins it is a safe bet (though not a certainty) that the excuses are not really as good as I think: as regards other men's sins against me it is a safe bet (though not a certainty) that the excuses are better than I think.[6]

Our unhealthy tendencies to take offense and offend take their toll on our relationships—oftentimes the relationship we value most. Our quickness to take umbrage and our reticence to forgive bring strain in even our best relationships. We try to mask it, but somehow our inner person is discernible. This unforgiving spirit, in turn, brings isolation and a compounding of our bitterness. It shows.

Self-pity finds its roots here. Then comes depression, as an unforgiving, offended self turns inward. We become even more fault-finding and "hurt" and unforgiving and depressed. This is all emotionally unhealthy. Not only do friendships sour, but our own healthy relationship with God becomes insipid. The heavens seem as brass to the unforgiving heart, and they practically are so. We suffer from spiritual ill-health.

On the other hand, the health benefits of a forgiving spirit are incalculable. The chief benefit is this: we are never closer to God, or more like God, than when we forgive. When we forgive, we are performing a function that has its origin in heaven. When we forgive, we are like the Father. When we forgive, we are like the Son, who called to God *in extremis*, "Father, forgive them; for they know not what they do" (Luke 23:34, KJV).

We say, "to err is human," and that is true. But the last part of that couplet is, "to forgive is divine." And so it is. We are never more beautiful and more noble and healthy than when we forgive, for we are then like God. Some of us need to believe that.

Some of us think that we are never more noble than when we say with General Oglethorpe: "I never forgive. And I'm so proud of my hatreds, and no one crosses me, and I always pay accounts." To forgive is divine; to not forgive is demonic.

This fifth petition of the Lord's Prayer is, as Augustine said, "a terrible petition," but it is also a gracious prayer. It cuts through all the evangelical jargon. And for Christians it is "terribly gracious," because it monitors our spiritual health. Are we healthy, forgiving people?

A Prayer for Forgiveness

Let us now touch briefly on the primary thrust of this fifth petition, which is forgiveness of sin. *"Forgive us our debts as we forgive our debtors"* is primarily a prayer for forgiveness.

The fundamental qualification for praying this prayer is that we are debtors—that is, sinners. It is probably true that most people who repeat this prayer today do not see themselves as sinners. People often pray the Lord's Prayer with a condescending tolerance that permits them to inwardly say, "I'm praying this along with the people who really need it." Thousands who say this prayer do not see themselves as debtors or trespassers or offenders. They don't consider themselves guilty before God.

So often, the Lord's Prayer is nothing more than an empty repetition by a self-satisfied soul. The fact is, it can be properly prayed only by "debtors." Are we debtors? I realize that most of us are Christians and that our sins have been paid for—past, present, and future—by the blood of Christ. I realize that we are called in the pure sense to confess them, for they are already eternally forgiven (1 John 1:9).

We don't need to excise the word "forgiveness" from our vocabulary, for this prayer teaches that we are to have a daily, ongoing awareness of sin which is accompanied by regular confession. In fact, confession is a sign of spiritual maturity. Healthy believers daily confess their sins.

In sum, this fifth petition, *"Forgive us our debts as we forgive our debtors,"* tells us to do two things. First, we are to ask God to forgive us. This request for forgiveness follows the request for daily food in the Lord's Prayer, and numerous commentaries have noted that it should at least equal or actually surpass our craving for food. I urge us all that if we have not yet had our debts canceled and forgiven, we ought to deal with them before we take our next meal. We must ask God to forgive us by the grace and blood of Jesus Christ. I don't know how to say it strongly enough—do it today!

The second thing this fifth petition tells us is to forgive those who have wronged us. And here again, the importance of doing this cannot be overstressed. We do this for the health of our soul. If we forgive, we will avoid a thousand ailments—and that is not hyperbole. We do it for the health of the church. The church is sick from want of forgiveness among its children. We do it for the sake of the world. The world has not yet discovered what Christ is like. But it can, if we will truly forgive—for "to forgive is divine."

Resolve to practice forgiving now. Do we need to forgive our spouse? Covenant to do it right now. Have we been unwilling to forgive our parents? We can promise God right now that we will do it. Tell Him when. Have we forgiven our employer who wronged us? We need to do it now—and we can. Do we have a grudge against our last church? Its pastor, its elders? Forgive today!

We must do it for our sake, the church's sake, and the world's sake. Forgiveness is not a psychological trick. It is a miracle. And God can help us do it. Do it for God's sake. Ephesians 4:32 says: "And be kind to one another, tender-hearted, forgiving each other, just as God in Christ also has forgiven you."

This is a "terrible petition." It can curse us or bless us. Dare we pray it? Can we pray it? *"Lord, forgive us our debts as we forgive our debtors. Amen."*

7

OUR DELIVERANCE

L ife has its way of making the Lord's Prayer become increasingly relevant with the passing of
years, and this is particularly true in respect to the
final petition, which has to do with temptation.

The seasons of life have, along with great joy,
brought vast personal disappointment due to the
shipwrecked lives of fellow believers. Men and
women who have borne the same weapons in spiritual battle, brothers and sisters whose heartbeats
were united with mine in love for Christ, have
fallen to temptation—bringing disgrace and sorrow
to Christ and His church.

I say this to underscore two things. The first is:
no one is above falling. No one is above shelving his
or her faith, family, and heritage. No one is above
yielding to temptation in its multiple, variegated
forms—no one! The pastor in his pressed suit and
starched shirt, who appears to "have it all together,"
is not above succumbing. None of us is, regardless
of our present spiritual temperature.

Second: *we need to know how to pray for spiritual protection for ourselves.*

And, of course, that is what the sixth and final petition of the Lord's Prayer is all about: *"Lead us not into temptation, but deliver us from evil"* (Matthew 6:13, KJV). The six petitions of the Lord's Prayer are structured like a ladder. The top three rungs are in heaven. The top rung prays regarding God's name—Father, the next rung down for the kingdom, the third down for His will.

The next three rungs descend to earth as we pray for our bread, then forgiveness, and finally, in this last petition, for protection from evil.

On the ladder of the Lord's Prayer we descend from the contemplation of who God is—His blessed Fatherhood—to who we are—vulnerable children. No prayer life is complete without this last rung, no matter how exalted and "spiritual" it is. Proper prayer includes praying for spiritual protection.

This final petition divides up into two requests. The first is negative: *"Lead us not into temptation,"* and the second is positive: *" . . . but deliver us from evil."*

Asking That God Will Not Lead Us into Temptation

The question is, what does *"Lead us not into temptation"* mean? Certainly it cannot mean (as some have wrongly thought) that God is the prime mover behind all temptations. James 1:13 makes this clear: "Let no one say when he is tempted, 'I am being tempted by God,' . . . He himself does not tempt anyone."

On the other hand, others have imagined that if Christians truly pray this prayer they can be delivered from *all* temptation. That is impossible because temptation is an integral part of human existence. All the apostles and all the great saints have lived in continual temptation.

The key to the meaning of *"Lead us not into temptation"* is that the word "temptation" has two meanings. It can mean a temptation which has the goal of causing one to sin; or it can mean a test or trial of the validity of one's faith. The word occurs twenty-one times in the New Testament, and twenty of those occurrences have the latter idea of testing or trial.[1]

Thus the meaning of *"Lead us not into temptation"* is simply this: "Don't allow us to come under the sway of temptation that will overpower us and cause us to sin." This interpretation is supported by an ancient Jewish evening prayer which Jesus may well have known:

> Lead me not into the power of transgression,
> And bring me not into the power of sin,
> And not into the power of iniquity,
> And not into the power of temptation,
> And not into the power of anything shameful.[2]

The idea is: "Lord, preserve me from temptation that will bring me under its sway and cause me to fall." The fact is, we can't help being exposed to temptation. We are not to pray that we will be spared it. Rather, we are to pray that we will be spared those temptations from Satan which we cannot withstand.

The abiding reality is that temptation is good for us. Temptation molded the life and ministry of the Lord Jesus Christ Himself. His ministry began with His epic temptations in the wilderness. Satan came at Him with the consummate psycho-spiritual attack. Jesus withstood it all, and with these paradigm temptations conquered, went on to live His peerless life.

Then, some three-and-a-half years later, His life ended as He triumphed *again* over temptation, when He conquered the impulse to flee from the cross in Gethsemane. The writer of Hebrews bears testimony to the molding effect of these and other sufferings as he writes in 2:10: "For it was fitting for Him, for whom are all things, and through whom are all things, in bringing many sons to glory, to perfect the author of their salvation through sufferings."

If temptations helped shape the life and ministry of Christ, so much more do they for us. Temptation is necessary for the development of our moral character. "Temptation is not so much the penalty of manhood as it is the glory of manhood. It is that by which a man is made an athlete of God."[3]

That was the way it was for Martin Luther. No one can doubt that Luther became stronger as he fought off the massive temptations of the world, the flesh, and the Devil. Temptation conquered knits the fibers of our souls into muscular cords. The old belief that the strength of the slain enemy passed into the slayer is true in regard to a Christian's overcoming temptations.

That is why the Scriptures urge the long view. "Consider it all joy, my brethren, when you encounter various trials, knowing that the testing of your faith produces endurance" (James 1:2, 3). That is why today we count among the great Christians of our time people like Dietrich Bonhoeffer, Corrie ten Boom, and Alexander Solzhenitsyn. Their great trials knit together the moral fiber of their souls.

The proper prayer regarding temptation is not that we be delivered from all temptation, for temptation, trials, and testing are necessary for the health of our souls. The proper prayer asks God to deliver us from overpowering temptations, because we are weak and liable to fold under severe testing. It was Peter's fleshly presumption that led to his terrible failure. You remember on the night of his fall he said, "I don't know about the rest of these mortals, but, God, you are looking at a superman. When all the rest of them forsake You, I'll never forsake You.

You see, God, I can stand." Then he denied Christ in sweaty, sordid, foul language that hadn't come from his lips in years.

Our presumption can take many forms. It can be prideful presumption that says, "I have grown so far in the Christian life, I can't fall." Or the pious presumption that says, "Yes, I am weak, I can fall," but does not really believe it. We need to see our weakness.

History records the fate of two men who were condemned to die in the burning days of Queen Mary. One of them boasted very loudly to his companions of his confidence that he would stand firm at the stake. He did not mind the suffering; he was so grounded in the gospel that he knew he would never deny it. He said that he longed for the fatal morning even as a bride for the wedding.

His companion in prison in the same chamber was a poor trembling soul who could not and would not deny his Master; but he told his companion that he was very much afraid of the fire. He said he had always been very sensitive to suffering, and he was in great dread that when he began to burn, the pain might cause him to deny the truth. He besought his friend to pray for him, and he spent his time in very much weeping over his weakness and in crying to God for strength. The other continually rebuked him and chided him for being so unbelieving and weak.

When they both came to the stake, he who had been so bold recanted at the sight of the fire and went back ignominiously to an apostate's life, while the poor trembling man whose prayer had been *"Lead me not into temptation"* stood firm as a rock, praising and magnifying God as he was burnt to a cinder.[4]

The proper prayer for protection is soaked with the awareness that we are all profoundly weak and liable to fall. There is a danger in the pious bravado that can come on us when we think we have arrived. That is the negatively stated aspect of the petition.

Asking That God Will Deliver Us from Evil

The Lord goes on to say, *"Deliver us from evil."* Here *The Living Bible, The New English Bible,* and the *New International Version* are very helpful, because they correctly render it, *"Deliver us from the evil one"*—referring, of course, to the Devil. The sense is clearly "Deliver us from the Devil."

And here is the point: proper prayer for spiritual protection understands that the Devil is a real person—not an impersonal cosmic force.

We all know that believing in a real Devil has not been in vogue for the last seventy-five years. Those who believe that there is an utterly malig-

nant being behind the universe's evil are sometimes classified as medieval fools. Antagonists
like to caricature those who believe in Satan as
thinking of him as a green-eyed fiend with cloven
hooves who smells like brimstone. The "in thing"
has been to pooh-pooh his existence, which, as
C. S. Lewis has said, is one of the best things the
forces of evil ever accomplished for themselves.

Fortunately, in recent years a return to Bible
reading, books like Lewis's *The Screwtape Letters,*
and the realities of evil in modern history have
done much to clear up people's thinking. As the
great theologian Helmut Thielicke said in post-
war, occupied Germany:

> . . . there is a dark, mysterious, spellbinding
> figure at work. Behind the temptations stands
> *the* tempter, behind the lie stands *the* liar, be-
> hind all the dead and bloodshed stands *the*
> "murderer from the beginning."

And then a few lines later he added, "Dear
friend, in our times we have had far too much
contact with demonic powers."[5]

The Scriptures call this malignant being "Satan" and "the Devil." "Satan" is the common
Hebrew word for *adversary,* as in 1 Samuel 29:4
where David is called a *satan* ("adversary") to the
Philistines. "Devil" is the common Greek word
for *slanderer,* as in 1 Timothy 3:11 where Paul

says women are to be serious-minded, not *dia-bolous,* "devils," "slanderers."

The Evil One is both our real adversary and our real slanderer. Moreover, he is a being of cosmic intelligence and stealth. He is dangerous precisely because he does not have hooves nor smell like sulphur. If we were to list his characteristics, we would have to write "none," except the effect of his work. That is the same whether it is in a prison or in the suburbs.

The point is, proper prayer acknowledges his amazing power. He is the prince of the power of the air, "the spirit that is now working in the sons of disobedience" (Ephesians 2:2). His agents are everywhere—in Washington, in Moscow, in seminary, in pulpits. He is not ubiquitous, but he tries to imitate the omnipresence of God by commanding a host of evil spirits that afflict the godly and the ungodly, even as God sends His ministering spirits to care for His elect. Second Corinthians 11:14, 15 says: "And no wonder, for even Satan disguises himself as an angel of light. Therefore it is not surprising if his servants also disguise themselves as servants of righteousness; whose end shall be according to their deeds."

But when we acknowledge his cosmic power in correctly praying *"Deliver us from the Evil One,"* we are, in the same breath, acknowledging that God's power is greater. God can deliver us! Luther was right when he sang:

The Prince of Darkness grim,
We tremble not for him,
His rage we can endure,
For lo, his doom is sure;
One little word shall fell him.

The proper prayer for spiritual protection is "Deliver us from the *evil one.*" It confirms Satan's power; it confirms our weakness; it confirms God's greater power.

"Deliver us" should be a part of our daily prayers. On my own prayer list I have a note that says, "spiritual warfare." There I pray regularly that God will put a hedge around our church, a hedge around my family, and then I list in pencil different ones who I know are undergoing the attacks of Satan and I pray they will be delivered from his power, his person, his emissaries. The daily prayer life of a believer has to include this if it is to fit the model.

The tragic demise of good Christians who have fallen by the wayside is not very unusual, is it? Many of us could relate tragedies which sadden us and our Savior. The path from Christ's way to "my way" is well traveled.

None of us is above succumbing to the trials and temptations that beset us. And the assaults come from everywhere: the images which assail our eyes, the incessant assaults on our senses, even from our own memories. We need to be in contact with our frailty and weakness and seek God's power, understanding that it is indispensable.

We do need to know how to pray for spiritual protection. While we understand that temptation is necessary for our spiritual growth, we must pray that God will keep us from temptations that would destroy us. We must humbly pray, *"Lead us not into temptation."* We must empty ourselves of all our spiritual presumption.

We must also pray, *"Deliver us from the evil one."* We must acknowledge that victory over Satan can come only through God's power. We are called to a profound dependence on God.

The bottom line is this: the capacity to authentically pray *"Lead us not into temptation, but deliver us from evil"* is a key to spiritual health. It is part of our Lord's ideal pattern for prayer. Do we pray it? Is a prayer for deliverance from temptation and the power of the Devil part of our everyday prayer? Are we willing to make it so?

If so, then we, like Jesus, can expect the angels to come and minister to us—much as they did for our Lord in the wilderness and in Gethsemane.

Pray then in this way: *"Lead us not into temptation, but deliver us from the evil one. Amen."*

8

GOD's
GLORY

We conclude our study on the Lord's Prayer with the closing doxology, *"For Thine is the kingdom, and the power, and the glory, forever. Amen."*

There is no ground whatsoever to suppose that this doxology was spoken by Christ as part of the original Lord's Prayer. The reasons are several, the foremost being that the doxology does not appear in any of the oldest manuscripts of Matthew. You will find that consistently the best and oldest manuscripts end the Lord's Prayer with *"deliver us from evil."* It appears that this doxology was added during the first or second century.

The earliest reference to the doxology comes from the *Didache,* or *Teaching of the Twelve Apostles,* which reproduces the Lord's Prayer and then adds these words, " . . . for thine is the power and the glory for ever. Pray thus three times a day."[1]

Ernst Lohmeyer, who has done one of the most scholarly and exhaustive studies of the Lord's Prayer, says that this doxology was included because of the Jewish custom of ending all daily prayers with a brief doxology. What happened, he says, is that the Jewish Christians in Syria began to repeat the Lord's Prayer daily with the customary addition of a doxology, finally adding it to their version of their New Testament—and from there it influenced other ancient versions.[2]

I think Lohmeyer's explanation makes good sense. From a literary point of view, one can also see why the doxology was included. It seems rather cold and cheerless to end the prayer with the word *"evil,"* while the doxology appears to form a more polished conclusion to the prayer.

But as we all know, the text of the Bible is not to be decided by one's feelings or notions of appropriateness, but by the evidence. And the evidence does not allow us to imagine that the doxology is part of the original Lord's Prayer as it came from the lips of Jesus.

However, it does not follow that because Jesus did not use it, it is wrong to insert the early church's song of praise at the end of the Lord's Prayer. The Lord's Prayer is an outline, a model, of what our prayers should contain. And there is nothing wrong with additional praise and doxology which is in keeping with the spirit of the prayer—as long as we do not imagine that Jesus said it.

Actually, the doxology is Scriptural in the sense that variations of it are found numerous times in the Bible. The Old Testament contains what many believe is the model from which this doxology is condensed. The reference is 1 Chronicles 29:10, 11, where David gives thanks before the whole people, saying: "Blessed art Thou, O Lord God of Israel our father, forever and ever. Thine, O Lord, is the greatness and power and the glory and the victory and the majesty. . . ."

In the New Testament, among the many parallel references are the words of the four living creatures in Revelation 5:13: "To Him who sits on the throne, and to the Lamb, be blessing and honor and glory and dominion forever and ever." So the doxology is Scriptural in content, and what we have in its un-Scriptural addition at the end of the Lord's Prayer is the church's proper "knee-jerk" reaction to praying the Lord's Prayer. The doxology is the joyous declaration of one who has truly prayed the Lord's Prayer.

> *For Thine is the kingdom!*—Lord!
> *Thine is the power!*—God!
> *Thine is the glory forever! Amen!*

We can, therefore, use this doxology, this human addition, as a model of the heart's response of the one who truly enters into the Lord's Prayer. It is the song, the declaration, of the heart that prays after the Lord's pattern of prayer. The declaration begins joyfully and impressively by saying, *"Thine is the kingdom."*

The Doxology Declares
the Kingdom to Be God's

The fundamental, underlying meaning of *"Thine is the kingdom"* is that God is King. The phrase carries the traditional Jewish sense of "Thou art king forever."[3] There is no truth that is more constantly reiterated in Scripture than "the Lord, He is King!"

"Thine is the kingdom" is a joyful affirmation of the sovereignty of God. It affirms that He is all-powerful, of which the next declaration of the doxology speaks. It affirms that He is all-knowing. In the most arresting of theological terms:

God knows instantly and effortlessly all matter and all matters, all mind and every mind, all spirit and all spirits, all being and every being, all creaturehood and all creatures, every plurality and all pluralities, all law and every law, all relations, all causes, all thoughts, all mysteries, all enigmas, all feeling, all desires, every unuttered secret, all thrones and dominions, all personalities, all things visible and invisible in heaven and in earth, motion, space, time, life, death, good, evil, heaven, and hell.

Because God knows all things perfectly, He knows no thing better than any other thing, but all things equally well. He never discovers anything. He is never surprised, never amazed. He never wonders about anything. . . .[4]

"Thine is the kingdom" also affirms that God is absolutely free. His freedom is beyond human ex-

perience and understanding. Our earthly analogies fall short of describing His freedom. We customarily describe someone whom we think is free as "free as a bird." But as any naturalist knows, a bird isn't free at all, for it is caged by its hungers and fears and instincts. Predators, food supplies, and the "territorial imperative" keep it in bondage.

Only God is free! He can do what He pleases when He pleases as He pleases. He is King!

But *"Thine is the kingdom"* affirms more than His sovereign kingship—it declares that He is King of this fallen, rebellious world. The world has trouble believing this. Everywhere one looks, it appears that only the strong and nasty prevail. As Napoleon said in a moment of vain cynicism, "I have observed that God is always on the side of the strongest battalions."[5]

Pontius Pilate reasoned along the same lines as he faced the mutilated visage of Christ, who was standing on the pavement before his palace, and cried to the crowd, "Behold, the Man!" (John 19:5). The power of Rome stood with Pilate. Jesus was to him no more than a twig on the unfortunate tides of history. And Jesus' words, "My kingdom is not of this world" (John 18:36) were incomprehensible to him.

The truth is, Pilate was the captive, and Jesus was the King, the only free man in history. Pilate's problem was that he was standing on the outside. He needed spiritual life to see the truth—

the eyes of Christ, so to speak.

If we do not see Christ as King and have experienced none of His kingdom, it is because we, too, are standing in the wrong place.

It is like the colored windows of a church. If you go around the outside of the church, you see nothing but gray monochrome and cannot tell whether they are merely dirty, sooty panes or works of art. In other words, you are seeing them from the wrong perspective. But the moment you enter the nave of the church, the windows begin to shine and the whole story of salvation, captured in color, rises up before you.[6]

The mystery of God's kingdom can be seen only from the inside. From within we joyously declare, *"Thine is the kingdom."* We are also aware that His kingdom is coming so that all will see it, even those on the outside, when He comes riding on a white horse, His name emblazoned on His robe and thigh, "KING OF KINGS, AND LORD OF LORDS" (Revelation 19:16).

We believe that He is in control, and that we will answer to Him—and this belief influences everything. Over three hundred and fifty years ago, Lancelot Andrewes sat as bishop of the Church of England. He was a marvelous preacher, and on a memorable occasion in 1621 he had the occasion to preach to the assembled House of Commons at their opening session. The Commons assembled before him in Westminster Abbey. He told his country's leaders that God was standing in the congregation and that God would judge among them; and that if they could see Him standing among them, they would never have to fear His judgment because their lives would be practically elevated. They needed just four things, said Andrewes:

> "1. Set down this and believe it, that He is present;
> 2. So behave yourselves as if you did believe it;
> 3. Show yourselves well affected to His presence;
> 4. Do those things which may make Him rejoice to be among you."[7]

Andrewes called the politicians of his day to live out what they publicly subscribed to—that God is King.

We must live believing God is King and His kingdom is now and is coming! Let us believe it. Let us proclaim together, *"Thine is the kingdom."*

Lord of every thought and action,
   Lord to send, and Lord to stay,
Lord in speaking, writing, giving,

Lord in all things to obey,
Lord of all there is of me,
   Now and evermore to be.[8]

That is the first thing we declare.

The Doxology Declares
That the Power Is God's

The second declaration of this doxology is *"Thine is the power."* As I mentioned, sovereignty and omnipotence must go together. One cannot exist without the other. To reign, God must have power. And to reign sovereignly, He must have all power. Omnipotent means simply this: all-powerful. God possesses an incomprehensible store of power.

That God is omnipotent ought to be self-evident truth for anyone in the Judeo-Christian tradition, but unfortunately it isn't so. Over a year ago a book appeared which rose to the top of the best-seller charts. The book is authored by Harold Kushner, a once obscure rabbi, and is entitled, *When Bad Things Happen to Good People.* The book deals with the age-old question, how can a God of love permit the horrible suffering and misery we see in this world? Kushner's answer is this: God is all-loving, but not all-powerful; the evil things that happen are simply out of His control.

Amazingly, people have been swallowing his

answer "hook, line, and sinker." One reader responded, "Maybe now I can believe in a *more realistic God.*" People welcome the idea of an omni-impotent God. Such ideas are not new. But what is amazing is that Christians are accepting this! A well-known pastor has endorsed it, and I'm told the book can be found in some Christian bookstores. So, folks, God isn't dead—He is just sick and feeble![9]

This chapter is not about the problem of evil, but I should say that the problem has been admirably dealt with in several recent books, with perhaps the best of them being Philip Yancey's masterful *Where Is God When It Hurts?* The Christian, Biblical answer is far superior and better argued than Kushner's "sick God" theory or the popular dualism of others. I hope that none of us will fall into such weak-minded foolishness. Some may get applause at a talk show for such views, but they will get no support from the Scriptures.

Psalm 62:11 expresses the truth beautifully: "Once God has spoken; twice I have heard this: that power belongs to God." The Old Testament refers to God as "Almighty" fifty-six times in the English text—and not once does it ascribe that title to any other being.

The New Testament is equally consistent and clear. Colossians 1:15-18 says: "And he is the image of the invisible God, the first-born of all creation. For in Him all things were created, both in the heavens and on earth, visible and invisible, whether thrones or dominions or rulers or authorities—all things have been created through Him and for Him. And He is before all things, and in Him all things hold together. He is also head of the body, the church; and He is the beginning, the first-born from the dead; so that He Himself might come to have first place in everything."

Romans 1:20 makes similar forceful claims: "For since the creation of the world His invisible attributes, His eternal power and divine nature, have been clearly seen, being understood through what has been made, so that they are without excuse."

And Revelation 19:6 (KJV) also corroborates God's power: "And I heard as it were the voice of a great multitude, and as the voice of many waters, and as the voice of mighty thunderings, saying, Alleluia: for the Lord God omnipotent reigneth."

Since God is omnipotent, He can do one thing as easily as anything else. All His acts are done without effort. He puts out no energy which must be replaced. He needs no renewal of strength because He is all strength. When we pray *"Thine is the power"* we are declaring that He can do anything.

If we do not believe this, we have no reason

to pray. If He is not omnipotent, then our prayers are exercises in pious futility. Do we really believe God is omnipotent? If not, be consistent—be honest. Stop praying. *"Thine is the power"* is the proper reflex from truly praying the Lord's Prayer. The six petitions all require an omnipotent God. *"Thine is the power,"* truly believed, brings a profound dependence upon Him. The Second Person of the Trinity tells us, "Apart from Me you can do nothing" (John 15:5). That is profoundly true.

But the converse is also true: with God we can do great things. On one of his canvases, the French painter Emile Ranouf has depicted an old man dressed in fisherman's garb, seated in a boat with a little girl beside him. Both the elderly man and the child have their hands on the huge oar. He is looking down fondly and admiringly upon her. Apparently he has told her that she may assist him in rowing the boat, and the child feels she is doing a great share of the task. It is easy to see, however, that it is his strong muscular arms which are actually propelling the boat through the waves. The painting is called, "A Helping Hand."

That is a parable of what a soul can do when it depends upon God. It is God's hand that propels us through life, even through storms, and accomplishes things for Him. So we say, *"Thine is the power"*—all power is Yours, we are dependent upon You, God. That is the reflex of the heart that knows the reality of the Lord's Prayer. Let us affirm that as we say it, *"Thine is the power."*

The Doxology Declares the Glory to Be God's

The doxology now rises to its final declaration: *"Thine is the glory."* When we think of God's glory, we must think of two things. First, His splendorous existence in light—the brightness which no human can bear. This is the "shekinah" glory of which Moses saw the "afterglow" as God covered him with His hand when His glory passed by. This is the glory that momentarily flowed through Jesus on the Mount of Transfiguration when His face flashed as the sun and His clothing became white with light.

Second, when we think of glory we must simply think of honor. Both of these infinitely belong to God. *"Thine is the glory"* is a martial-like shout that all splendor and all honor be God's.

It is intensified by the addition of the word *"forever."* How long is forever? An illustration has been with me since I was a boy, and I have fed on it time and time again. It is this: If I were to hold a dove in my hand and I could tell it to fly to the moon, gather some moondust in its tiny beak, and fly back here and deposit it at my feet, in the time the dove, after repeated flights, delivered all of the moon to my feet, eternity would have just begun.

Moreover, when we say *"Thine is the glory forever,"* we are not talking about a static existence. The phrase used here in the Greek for "forever" reads literally "into the ages." The Hebrew idea, as opposed to the Greek idea of a timeless state, is an eternity of unfolding ages.

We joyfully declare in faith, *"Thine is the glory,"* for glory will be God's always. But the miracle is, we will share in the glory! In 2 Corinthians 4:16, 17 we read: "Therefore we do not lose heart, but though our outer man is decaying, yet our inner man is being renewed day by day. For momentary, light affliction is producing for us an eternal weight of glory far beyond all comparison."

As we remember that His is the glory, we are called to resist the "sorcery of things"—our material fixations—and seek the things which are eternal. The proper reflex of the heart which prays the Lord's Prayer is to declare, *"Thine is the glory."* Let us declare it together!

To this we conclude, *"Amen,"* which is the Hebrew way of saying, "Let it be so"—"so be it." But here it means even more. It is a confident expression that all this *will* be so. It is a word of faith and conviction.

Think once more of the ladder of the Lord's Prayer. Its first three rungs extend from heaven, and as we back down them we pray for:

His name: *"Hallowed be Thy name."*
His kingdom: *"Thy kingdom come."*
His will: *"Thy will be done on earth as it is in heaven."*

The bottom three rungs extend up from earth, from mortals. And as we descend these we pray for:

Our food: *"Give us this day our daily bread."*
Our forgiveness: *"And forgive us our debts as we forgive our debtors."*
Our vulnerability: *"And lead us not into temptation, but deliver us from evil."*

As we truly pray this pattern, as our prayers more and more contain these six elements, we will increasingly rise with the early church to the joyous doxology: *"For Thine is the kingdom, and the power, and the glory, forever. Amen."*

NOTES

1. James Boice, *The Sermon on the Mount* (Grand Rapids, Mich.: Zondervan, 1972), p. 192.
2. Dietrich Bonhoeffer, *The Cost of Discipleship* (New York: Macmillan, 1969), p. 184.

Chapter One: God the Father
1. Joachim Jeremias, *The Lord's Prayer* (Philadelphia: Fortress Press, 1980), pp. 19, 20.
2. *Ibid.,* p. 20.
3. J. I. Packer, *Knowing God* (Downers Grove, Ill.: InterVarsity Press, 1973), p. 182.
4. Everett Fullam, *Living the Lord's Prayer* (Grand Rapids, Mich.: Chosen Books, 1980), pp. 27, 28.

Chapter Two: God's Name
1. Nels Ferre, *Strengthening the Spiritual Life* (London: Collins, 1956), p. 1.
2. William Barclay, *The Beatitudes and Lord's Prayer*

for Everyman (New York: Harper and Row, 1964), p. 179.
3. *Ibid.,* pp. 187, 188.

Chapter Three: God's Kingdom
1. John R. W. Stott, *Christian Counter-Culture* (Downers Grove, Ill.: InterVarsity Press, 1978), p. 147.
2. Ernst Lohmeyer, *Our Father* (New York: Harper and Row, 1965), p. 104.
3. Quoted by James Boice, *The Sermon on the Mount* (Grand Rapids, Mich.: Zondervan, 1972), p. 208.
4. Helmut Thielicke, *Our Heavenly Father* (Grand Rapids, Mich.: Baker Book House, 1980), p. 60.
5. *Ibid.,* p. 62.
6. *Ibid.,* p. 57.
7. Donald W. Dayton, *Discovering an Evangelical Heritage* (New York: Harper and Row, 1976), pp. 8-10.

Chapter Four: God's Will
1. Helmut Thielicke, *Our Heavenly Father* (Grand Rapids, Mich.: Baker Book House, 1980), p. 70, 71.
2. William Barclay, *The Beatitudes and the Lord's Prayer for Everyman* (New York: Harper and Row, 1975), p. 208.
3. Martin E. Marty, *The Hidden Discipline* (St. Louis, Mo.: Concordia, 1962), p. 73.

4. Elisabeth Elliot, "The Glory of God's Will," *World Vision* (April 1977), p. 12. Also available in booklet form, same title (Westchester, Ill.: Good News Publishers).
5. *Ibid.*, p. 13.

Chapter Five: Our Bread
1. Helmut Thielicke, *Our Heavenly Father* (Grand Rapids, Mich.: Baker Book House, 1980), pp. 77, 78.
2. William Barclay, *The Beatitudes and the Lord's Prayer for Everyman* (New York: Harper and Row, 1975), pp. 219, 220. See also Joachim Jeremias, *The Lord's Prayer* (Philadelphia: Fortress Press, 1980), pp. 23, 24.
3. *Op. cit.*, Thielicke, *Our Heavenly Father*, p. 79.
4. *Ibid.*, p. 81.
5. Ernst Lohmeyer, *Our Father* (New York: Harper and Row, 1965), p. 148. "And this thought is further underlined by the fact that while in the Old Testament there are many vivid pictures which paint the glory of the final kingdom, in the words of Jesus there is only one, which is drawn many times, the picture of the marriage feast or the king's feast, of eating and drinking or reclining at table with the patriarchs in Abraham's bosom, and the pictures of harvest or sowing only serve to show the great context in which 'our bread' is situated. One might almost say that from this point of view to pray for the

coming of the kingdom and to pray 'Give us our bread today' amounted to the same thing."

Chapter Six: Our Forgiveness
1. F. C. Cook, ed., *Speaker's Commentary* (New York: C. Scribner's, 1878-1896), p. 30.
2. Bruce M. Metzger, ed., *Oxford Annotated Apocrypha: Revised Standard Version* (Oxford, England: Oxford University Press, 1977), p. 164.
3. I. Thomas, ed., *Puritan Quotations* (Chicago: Moody Press, 1975), p. 111.
4. Charles Haddon Spurgeon, *The Metropolitan Tabernacle Pulpit,* 63 volumes, Vol. 24 (Pasadena, Tex.: Pilgrim Publications, 1969), p. 694.
5. C. S. Lewis essay in *Fern-seed and Elephants,* Walter Hooper, editor (Glasgow: Fontana/Collins, 1975), pp. 39, 40.
6. *Ibid.,* p. 42.

Chapter Seven: Our Deliverance
1. Joachim Jeremias, *The Lord's Prayer* (Philadelphia: Fortress Press, 1980), p. 29.
2. Jeremias, *The Lord's Prayer,* p. 30, quoting b, Berakoth 60b. in *The Babylonian Talmud,* p. 378.
3. William Barclay, *The Beatitudes and the Lord's Prayer for Everyman* (New York: Harper and Row, 1975), p. 247.
4. Charles Haddon Spurgeon, *The Metropolitan Tabernacle Pulpit,* 63 volumes, Vol. 24 (Pasadena, Tex.: Pilgrim Publications, 1969), p. 143.

5. Helmut Thielicke, *Our Heavenly Father* (Grand Rapids, Mich.: Baker, 1980), p. 133.

Chapter Eight: God's Glory

1. E. H. Warmington, ed., The Loeb Classical Library, *The Apostolic Fathers,* Vol. 1 (Harvard: Harvard University Press, 1970).
2. Ernst Lohmeyer, *Our Father* (New York: Harper and Row, 1965), pp. 230, 231.
3. *Ibid.,* p. 241.
4. A. W. Tozer, *The Knowledge of the Holy* (New York: Harper and Row, 1961), p. 62.
5. F. W. Farrar, *The Lord's Prayer* (New York: Thomas Whittaker, 1893), p. 221.
6. Helmut Thielicke, *Our Heavenly Father* (Grand Rapids, Mich.: Baker Book House, 1980), p. 152.
7. *Op. cit.,* Farrar, *The Lord's Prayer,* p. 217.
8. Alan Redpath, *Victorious Praying* (Old Tappan, N. J.: Revell, 1957), p. 127.
9. See Charles Colson, *Who Speaks for God?* (Westchester, Illinois: Crossway Books, 1985), pp. 21, 22.